GE

A

A quick beginners' course for holidaymakers and businesspeople

Course writers: Salah El-Ghobashy
Principal Lecturer in Arabic,
University of Westminster

Hilary Wise
Lecturer in Linguistics,
Queen Mary College,
University of London

Producer: Alan Wilding

BBC Books

Get by in Arabic
A BBC Radio course

Published to accompany a series of programmes prepared in consultation with BBC Continuing Education Advisory Council

Cover designed by
Peter Bridgewater and Annie Moss

Published by BBC Books,
a division of BBC Enterprises Limited,
Woodlands, 80 Wood Lane,
London W12 0TT

ISBN 0 563 39948 1
First published in 1985
Reissued 1988
Reprinted 1988
Reprinted 1989 (twice)
Reprinted 1990
Reprinted 1991
Reprinted 1993 (twice)
This edition published in 1995

Printed and bound in Great Britain
by Clays Ltd, St Ives plc
Cover printed by Clays Ltd, St Ives plc

Contents

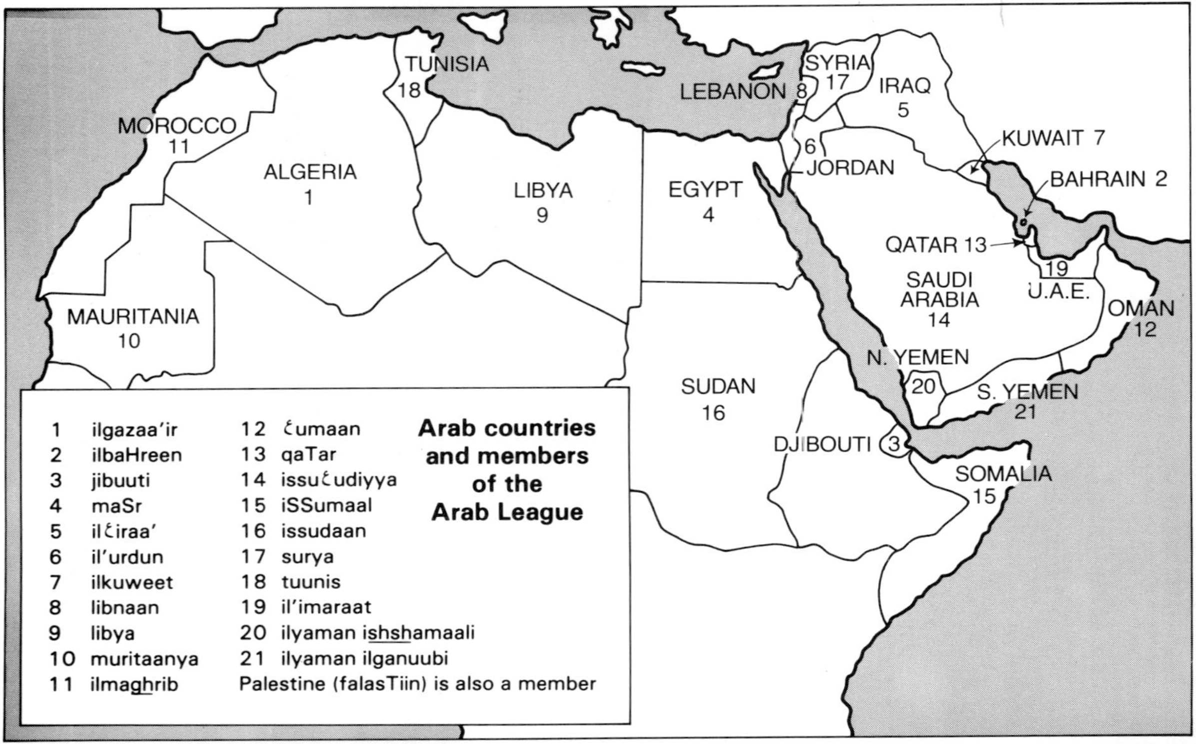
TUNISIA 18
MOROCCO 11
ALGERIA 1
LIBYA 9
EGYPT 4
LEBANON 8
SYRIA 17
IRAQ 5
6 JORDAN
KUWAIT 7
BAHRAIN 2
QATAR 13
19 U.A.E.
SAUDI ARABIA 14
OMAN 12
MAURITANIA 10
SUDAN 16
N. YEMEN 20
S. YEMEN 21
DJIBOUTI 3
SOMALIA 15
Arab countries and members of the Arab League
1 ilgazaa'ir
2 ilbaHreen
3 jibuuti
4 maSr
5 ilʿiraa'
6 il'urdun
7 ilkuweet
8 libnaan
9 libya
10 muritaanya
11 ilmaghrib
12 ʿumaan
13 qaTar
14 issuʿudiyya
15 iSSumaal
16 issudaan
17 surya
18 tuunis
19 il'imaraat
20 ilyaman ishshamaali
21 ilyaman ilganuubi
Palestine (falasTiin) is also a member

The course... and how to use it

Get by in Arabic is a six-programme radio course for anyone planning to visit an Arabic-speaking country. It offers a basic 'survival kit' for dealing with the kinds of situation likely to arise on a visit abroad and assumes no previous knowledge of the language.

About Arabic

About 180 million people speak Arabic as their first language. As the language of the Koran, it is also learnt by many millions of Moslems throughout the world.

Arabic is sometimes thought to be a 'difficult' language, perhaps because it is written in an unfamiliar script. So in this book, we have used a writing system based on the Roman alphabet to represent the sounds of the language.

In Arab countries, courtesy and sociability are highly valued, and this is reflected in the language. It abounds in polite expressions, appropriate to particular situations, and any foreigner making the effort to speak Arabic will be welcomed with added warmth and hospitality.

What kind of Arabic?

There are basically two kinds of Arabic: literary and spoken. Literary Arabic is used as the written medium throughout the Arab world, and is spoken on the more formal occasions — in speeches, sermons, news broadcasts and so on. But for all everyday purposes — at home, in shops and offices — colloquial Arabic is used. The area of the Arab world is so vast (three times larger than the whole of Europe from Finland to Spain and from Ireland to Greece) that, not surprisingly, the language varies from country to country.

There are a number of reasons for choosing Egyptian Arabic. Geographically and historically Egypt lies at the heart of the Arab world. Its population (49 million) by far exceeds that of any other Arab country. Practically everyone in the Arab world is exposed, directly or indirectly, to Egyptian Arabic. Films, cassettes of popular songs and television soap operas are exported on a massive scale to other Arab countries. It is generally held to be the most prestigious spoken variety and whichever country you visit you will find people can understand and adapt to Egyptian Arabic.

However, the course also includes some non-Egyptian words which are in widespread use throughout the Arab world. These are given in the additional vocabulary and shown in square brackets.

The programmes

- are based on real-life conversations specially recorded in Cairo, so you get used to hearing everyday Arabic right from the start.
- enable you to cope with confidence in basic day-to-day situations such as meeting people, eating out, shopping and bargaining, travelling around, finding a room, making an appointment, and so on.

The book includes

- an introduction to the sounds of Arabic
- the key words and phrases for each programme
- the texts of the conversations in the order they appear in the programmes
- short explanations of the language
- extra useful vocabulary for each basic situation and background information about life in Arab countries

- exercises to test what you've learnt
- a reference section including language notes, the key to exercises, an introduction to the Arabic script for the really adventurous, and an Arabic-English word-list

The two cassettes

- contain an expanded form of the programmes and extra conversations and exercises. The key words in the 'Guide to pronunciation' section are given at the start of Cassette 1, so you can hear and imitate them while getting to know the writing system we have used; spoken answers to the exercises and test in this book are also given.
- give you the chance to go at your own pace, and take your study of the language a stage further, if you wish.

To make the most of the course

The way you use the course will depend on you and whether you're using the cassettes or the programmes or both. Here are some suggestions:

- If you have the cassettes, practise the key words given at the start of Cassette 1, which are printed on p12.

- *Before each programme,* look at the key words and phrases at the beginning of each chapter, and practise saying them aloud. Read the conversations aloud several times, with someone else if possible. Check the meaning of any words you don't know. Words appearing for the first time are given after the dialogues, otherwise you can check in the full word-list at the end of the book. Then read the explanations provided.

- *During each programme,* listen to the conversations *without looking at the book* and concentrate on the sounds of the language. When you're asked to repeat a word or phrase, try saying it aloud and confidently; this will help you to remember the expressions and to learn to say them with the proper stress. On the cassettes the pauses may seem a little short at first; if so, stop the tape.
- *After each programme,* read through the conversations aloud again. If you have the cassettes, you may find it useful to imitate the conversations phrase by phrase. Check again on the language explanations, then work through the exercises.
- *Making the most of the cassettes:* besides the dialogues and explanations expanding on the programmes, the cassettes contain additional conversations and exercises to reinforce what you've already learnt, and extend your vocabulary. Some of the exercises will draw on the additional vocabulary given at the end of each chapter. So if you make full use of the cassettes you can take your Arabic well beyond the stage of 'getting by'.

Guide to pronunciation

Arabic has its own alphabet of 28 letters, and an introduction to the Arabic script is given on p86. In this book, though, we have used a modified form of the Roman alphabet. The following is a guide to the written symbols we are using and the sounds they represent. The description of sounds relate to standard southern English.

Contrary to general belief, most of the sounds of Arabic are similar to those found in English; only about half a dozen will be unfamiliar to English speakers (and two of these occur relatively infrequently anyway).

- The vowels

There are three short vowels:

a like the vowel in English 'hat' or 'back', as in **gamal** (camel)

i like the vowel in 'hit' or 'ship', as in **bint** (girl)

u like the vowel in 'put' or 'hood', as in **shuft** (I saw)

and five long ones:

aa like a longer version of the vowel in 'met', as in **haat** (bring)

ii like the vowel in 'keen', as in **miin?** (who?)

uu like the vowel in 'food', as in **nuur** (light)

oo like the vowel in 'home', except the lips are rounder and tenser, as in **yoom** (day)

ee like the vowel in 'may' or 'lane', but with the lips more widely and tensely spread, as in **feen?** (where?)

- The consonants

The sounds represented by b, d, f, g, h, j, k, l, m, n, s, t, v, w, y, z are virtually identical to their English counterparts.

sh (underlined) represents the sound you find in 'shoot' or 'shop' and not the one in 'mishap'; eg **shaay** (tea)

r a 'rolled' r, made by vibrating the tip of the tongue behind the teeth, as in **wara** (behind)

S, T, D, Z represent 'heavy' or 'thick' versions of s, t, d, and z. They are pronounced with the muscles of the lips and the tongue very lax and loose, and can affect adjacent vowels, particularly aa, which is then pronounced more like the vowel in 'half'. Listen on the cassette to the difference in both the initial consonant and vowel in:

saami *(man's name)* and **Saafi** (pure)
taani (second) and **Taalib** (student)

- **kh** (underlined) like the final sound in Scottish 'loch', as in **khamsa** (five)
- **gh** (underlined) like the French 'r' sound (like a very brief gargle!), as in **ghaali** (expensive)
- **'** indicates a glottal stop, which you find a lot in Cockney English replacing a 't', as in 'bu'er' or 'Sco'land'. In Arabic it is a sound in its own right, and not an indication that something has been omitted. Eg **ma'aas** (size)
- **q** as in **ilqaahira** (Cairo) is similar to a 'k' sound, but produced further back, in about the same place as **gh**. It has the same effect on adjacent vowels as the 'thick' consonants.
- **H** represents a very aspirated 'h'. You can achieve it by pretending you have drunk something very hot, breathing out heavily over the back of your tongue. When you make this sound, you should be able to feel the friction at the back of your throat. Eg **Haaga** (thing)
- ع is an unfamiliar sound in English. It is somewhere between the glottal stop and the gh in ghaali, and is made with the whole of the tongue as far back as possible in the throat; as in **عala** (on)

Consonants, like vowels, may be long; we have indicated this by doubling the letter. You must pronounce these consonants as doubles, ie as in English 'smalllad' or 'commonname'.

Sala (prayer) **Salla** (he prayed)
ana (I) **fanni** (artistic)

The definite article (the) is **il-** and is joined to the noun:

kart (a card) **ilkart** (the card)

But when the noun begins with any of the following consonants:

t d n s z sh r T D S Z

the 'l' disappears and the first consonant is doubled and pronounced long:

nuur (light) **innuur** (the light)
raagil (a man) **irraagil** (the man)

In short words like **fi** (at, in), **wi** (and), **li** (to, for), the 'i' often disappears when another vowel precedes or follows:

talaata w nuSS (three and a half)
ilwalad w ilbint (the boy and the girl)
f ilqaahira (in Cairo)

If a word ends in two consonants and the next word begins with one, Egyptians often put in a short 'helping' vowel, to avoid the combination of three consonants in a row, which they find difficult. This is shown in the transcripts of the recorded conversations by an italic *i*, eg **nuSS*i* kiilu** (half a kilo).

It's important to stress a word in the right place; if the final vowel is long, it is stressed:

maZb**uu**T bar**ii**d

Otherwise the last syllable but one normally carries the stress:

mud**a**rris mudarr**i**sa

The few exceptions to the above are shown with a written accent, like this:

dáraga sálaTa

Finally, the best way of acquiring a reasonable pronunciation is to imitate the speakers in the programmes or the cassettes. You could also try saying aloud the key words at the beginning of each chapter, and then compare them with the native speaker's version. Best of all, of course, find an Egyptian to help you!

While you should try to be as accurate as possible in pronounciation, Arabic speakers are not only used to hearing a wide variety of accents from within the Arab world, they are also genuinely delighted to find a foreigner making an effort to speak Arabic.

Listen and repeat

The following word-list demonstrates the sounds of Arabic. The words are given at the start of Cassette 1.

Long vowels

haat miin yoom feen nuur

Thick consonants

saam Saam taab Taab daani Daani zaahir Zaahir

Other unfamiliar constants

r	raagil	bariid	kart
kh	khubz	khaalid	sukhna
gh	ghaali	baghdaad	ghani
q	qaasim	ilqaahira	qarya
k/q	kalb/qalb	kaam/qaam	
H	Haal	Hisaab	aHmad
h/H	haal/Haal	hadd/Hadd	
'	'ahwa	ba'shiish	la'
ع	عala	عaawiz	saعiid
'/ع	'amal/عamal	ma'aas/maعaad	'aal/عaal

Long consonants

sitta	iddiini	innuur
iTTaalib	issana	ishshanTa

Watch the stress

muh**a**ndis muhand**i**sa	itf**a**DDal itfaDD**a**li
T**aa**lib Taal**i**ba	kw**a**yyis kwayy**i**sa
Sugh**a**yyar Sughayy**a**ra	k**a**llim kall**i**mni

1 Meeting people

Key expressions

ahlan **ahlan wa sahlan**	hallo, nice to meet you
ahlan biik	*reply (to a man)*
ahlan biiki	*reply (to a woman)*
SabaaH ilkheer	good morning
SabaaH innuur	*reply*
misaa' ilkheer	good evening
misaa' innuur	*reply*
izzayyak?	how are you? (*to a man*)
izzayyik?	how are you? (*to a woman*)
ismak 'eeh?	what is your name? (*to a man*)
ismik 'eeh?	what is your name? (*to a woman*)
ismi shiriif	my name is shiriif
ana min landan	I am from London
ana muhandis	I am an engineer
maꜥa ssalaama	goodbye
ashuufak imta?	when will I see you? (*to a man*)
ashuufik imta?	when will I see you? (*to a woman*)

Conversations

1 Hello! How are you?

Two girls meet ...

zeenab	aah! naahid! izzayyik?
naahid	ilHamdu lillaah, kwayyisa. w inti, izzayyik?
zeenab	ana kwayyisa, ilHamdu lillaah.

In the morning two boys meet ...

Taari'	heey! SabaaH ilkheer!

shiriif SabaaH innuur ya Taari'! izzayyak?
Taari' ilHamdu lillaah, kwayyis. w izzayyak inta?
shiriif ilHamdu lillaah, kwayyis.

In the evening ...

Taari' heey! misaa' ilkheer.
muudi misaa' innuur.
Taari' izzayyak ya muudi?
muudi izzayyak inta?
Taari' ilHamdu lillaah, kwayyis, w inta?
muudi ilHamdu lillaah, kwayyis.

2 What's your name ...?

mu'nis ahlan.
'inaas ahlan biik.
mu'nis inti ismik 'eeh?
'inaas ana ismi 'inaas. w inta?
mu'nis ismi mu'nis.

3 ...and where are you from?

sanaa' ismak 'eeh?
shiriif ismi shiriif. w inti ismik 'eeh?
sanaa' ana ismi sanaa'.

shiriif	inti mineen, ya sanaa'?
sanaa'	ana min hina, min maSr. w inta mineen?
shiriif	ana min buur saعiid.
sanaa'	ahlan wa sahlan.
shiriif	ahlan biiki.

Taari' meets people from around the Arab world.

Taari'	misaa' ilkheer.
Man	misaa' innuur.
Taari'	inta mineen min faDlak?
Man	ana min issudaan, min ilkhartuum.
Man	...ana min iSSumaal.
Man	...ana min issuعudiyya.
Man	...ana min ilqaahira.
Man	...ana min 'aSwaan.
Man	...ana min nuuba.

4 What do you do ...?

Man	ana muhandis. w inta?
Man	ana mudiir bank.
Woman	ana mudarrisa. w inti?
Woman	ana duktuura.
Man	ana Taalib. w inta?
Man	ana Taalib kamaan.

5 Saying goodbye ...

zeenab and her friend arrange to meet the next day.

zeenab	ashuufik imta?
Friend	ashuufik bukra, in sha'allaah.
zeenab	bukra... hina?
Friend	'aywa, hina.
zeenab	maعa ssalaama.
Friend	maعa ssalaama.

Vocabulary

ana *I*
inta *you* (m)
inti *you* (f)
huwwa *he*
hiyya *she*
'aywa *yes*
la' *no*
wi *and*
kamaan *also*
ilHamdu lillaah *fine*
kwayyis *fine, well*
bi kheer *fine, well*
'eeh? *what?*
mineen? *where from?*
imta? *when?*
min *from*
hina *here*
maSr *Egypt, Cairo* (see p19)
buur saɛiid *Port Said*
'aSwaan *Aswan*
nuuba *Nubia (S. Egypt)*
iSSumaal *Somalia*
issudaan *Sudan*
issuɛudiyya *Saudi Arabia*
ilkhartuum *Khartoum*
ism *name*
ya used before person's name (see p17)
muhandis *engineer*
mudiir bank *bank manager*
mudarrisa *teacher* (f)
duktuura *doctor* (f)
Taalib *student*
ashuufik *I'll see you* (to a woman)
bukra *tomorrow*
in sha'allaah *God willing, I hope so*

Explanations

Arabic is rich in elaborate greetings, often with religious overtones. Here are a few of the commonest.

- Hello

  ahlan or **ahlan wa sahlan**
  Reply:
  ahlan or **ahlan biik** (to a man)
  ahlan biiki (to a woman)

- Good morning

  SabaaH ilkheer (*lit* morning of goodness)
  Reply:
  SabaaH ilkheer or **SabaaH innuur** (*lit* morning of light)
  'Morning' lasts till lunchtime, which may be at two or three o'clock.

- Good evening

  misaa' ilkheer
  Reply:
  misaa' ilkheer or **misaa' innuur**

- When talking directly to someone or calling them, you usually put **ya** in front of their name: **ahlan, ya huda.**

- How are you?

  izzayyak? (to a man)
  izzayyik? (to a woman)
  To be more emphatic, you can add the pronoun 'you' - **inta** to a man, **inti** to a woman:
  izzayyak inta? **izzayyik inti?**

- **wi** means 'and'. Notice the '**i**' disappears before another vowel: **w inta, izzayyak?**

- I'm fine ...

  kwayyis (if you're a man)
  kwayyisa (if you're a woman)
  Notice **-a** is usually added to adjectives and nouns to make them feminine.
  bi kheer is another way of saying 'fine', but it never changes.
  Almost always people add **ilHamdu lillaah** (*lit* praise be to God). In fact, it is often used alone without **kwayyis** or **bi kheer**.
  izzayyak? ilHamdu lillaah

- 'I' is **ana.**

  In a sentence like **ana kwayyisa** (I'm fine), **inta mineen?** (where are you from?) or **zeenab min maSr** (zeenab is from Egypt), there is no word equivalent to 'am', 'are' or 'is'.

- 'Name' is **ism**

  If you want to say 'my name' you add **-i**: **ismi shiriif.**
  'Your *(m)* name' is **ismak.**
  'Your *(f)* name' is **ismik.**

- 'What?' is **'eeh?** To ask someone their name:
  (to a woman) **ismik** | **'eeh?**
  (to a man) **ismak** |
  (*lit* your name is what?)
  Again, the pronouns 'I' and 'you' are often added for emphasis:
  inta ismak 'eeh? ana ismi shiriif

- 'Where from?' is **mineen?** Like **'eeh,** this follows the subject:
  inta mineen? huda mineen?
  To reply you use **min** (from) with the name of a place:
  ana min landan. huda min maSr.

- 'He' is **huwwa**. 'She' is **hiyya.**
  When using the feminine pronouns **hiyya** or **inti**, the noun or adjective must be feminine:
  huwwa duktuur he's a doctor
  hiyya duktuura she's a doctor
  huwwa kwayyis he's fine
  hiyya kwayyisa she's fine
  There's often a shift in stress when an 'a' is added:
  mud**a**rris, mudarr**i**sa; muh**a**ndis, muhand**i**sa

- To say goodbye ...

  maƐa ssalaama (with peace). The reply is the same.

- 'When?' is **imta?** To ask 'When shall I see you?':
  (to a woman) **ashuufik** | **imta?**
  (to a man) **ashuufak** | **imta?**

  You will hear **iṅ sha'allaah** (God willing) all the time; it almost automatically follows any reference to future plans (as in the last conversation: **ashuufik bukra, in sha'allaah** - 'I'll see you tomorrow, I hope'). With the right kind of slightly doubtful intonation, it can even be a polite way of saying no.

Additional vocabulary

briTanya *Britain*
amriika *America*
ingiltira *England*
iskotlanda *Scotland*
airlanda *Ireland*
weelz *Wales*
kánada *Canada*
ostralya *Australia*
ilhind *India*
bakistaan *Pakistan*
ilyabaan *Japan*
iSSiin *China*
rusya *Russia*
baraziil *Brazil*

See map on p4 for the names of all the Arab countries.
NB **maSr** is 'Egypt', but is also used colloquially for 'Cairo'. The formal name for Cairo is **ilqaahira.**

mudarris/mudarrisa	*teacher*
duktuur/duktuura	*doctor*
Taalib/Taaliba	*student*
muhandis/muhandisa	*engineer*
mudiir/mudiira	*manager, director*
SaHafi/SaHafiyya	*journalist*
khabiir/khabiira	*expert, consultant*
sikirteer/sikirteera	*secretary*
عaamil/عaamila	*worker*
sitt/ beet	*housewife*
raagil 'aعmaal	*businessman*
issalaamu عaleekum	(lit *Peace be upon you* - at any time of day)
عaleekum issalaam	Reply
marHaba	*Welcome*
marHaba biik	Reply (to a man)
marHaba biiki	Reply (to a woman)
keef Haalak?	*How are you?* (to a man)
keef Haalik?	*How are you?* (to a woman)
tiSbaH عala kheer	*Good night* (to a man)
tiSbaHi عala kheer	*Good night* (to a woman)

Exercises

1 Pretend your name is John, and you are from England (**ingiltira**). Now answer the following questions:

a inta mineen?
b ismak 'eeh?

2 Answer questions **a** and **b** again. This time you are Taari' from Cairo.

3 What time of day would you greet people in the following way:

a misaa' ilkheer
b SabaaH ilkheer
c ahlan wa sahlan

4 Give appropriate replies to **3a, b,** and **c.**

5 You are meeting shiriif for the first time.

a Say hallo and ask him his name.
b Now ask him where he's from.

6 You are meeting naahid for the first time.

a Say hallo and ask her her name.
b Now ask her where she is from.

7 You meet mu'nis, whom you already know.

a Say 'Good morning, mu'nis'.
b Ask him how he is.
c Ask him when you'll see him.
d When he suggests tomorrow, say 'I hope so'.

Mohamed Ali Mosque, Cairo

2 Food and drink

Key expressions

fiih عaSiir?	is there any juice?
mafiish biira hina	there's no beer here
عandak 'eeh?	what have you *(m)* got?
عandik 'eeh?	what have you *(f)* got?
ilHisaab, min faDlak	the bill, please
ana عaawiz	I *(m)* want
ana عawza	I *(f)* want
iddiini ...	give me ...
tishrab 'eeh?	what will you *(m)* drink?
tishrabi 'eeh?	what will you *(f)* drink?
shukran	thank you
عafwan; ilعafw	not at all

Conversations

1 Something to drink ...

Waiter	tishrab 'eeh?
Taari'	ashrab shaay.
Waiter	HaaDir.
Taari'	shukran.

2 zeenab is in a cafe.

Waiter	tishrabi 'eeh?
zeenab	عandak 'eeh?
Waiter	shaay walla 'ahwa walla Haaga saʼعa?
zeenab	'ahwa maZbuuT, min faDlak.
Waiter	HaaDir.

3 Two coffees, a tea and water pipe.

Waiter	SabaaH ilkheer. ayy*i* khidma?
Taari'	SabaaH innuur. iddiini itneen 'ahwa w waaHid shaay.
Waiter	(*shouting out to kitchen*) itneen 'ahwa, waaHid shaay!
Cook	HaaDir.
Taari'	(*calling after the waiter*) wi shiisha, min faDlak!

4 Many cafes don't sell alcoholic drinks ...

Taari'	ʿandak biira min faDlak?
Waiter	mafiish biira hina, ya beeh.
Taari'	shukran.
Waiter	ilʿafw, ya beeh.

5 ..but some of them do.

Taari'	ʿandak biira?
Waiter	'aywa, ʿandi biira.
Taari'	iddiini talaata biira min faDlak.
Waiter	HaaDir.
Taari'	(*later*) ilHisaab, min faDlak.
Waiter	'aywa.

6 Asking what juices there are.

zeenab	SabaaH ilkheer.
Waiter	SabaaH innuur.
zeenab	ʿandak ʿaSiir 'eeh, min faDlak?
Waiter	fiih ʿaSiir burTu'aan, fiih ʿaSiir gawaafa, fiih ʿaSiir manga, fiih ʿaSiir farawla, fiih ʿaSiir lamuun.
zeenab	ʿandak grepfruut?
Waiter	la', ʿaSiir grepfruut mafiish.
zeenab	waaHid gawaafa, min faDlak.
Waiter	HaaDir.

7 Asking what sandwiches they have ...

zeenab	SabaaH ilkheer.
Girl	SabaaH innuur.

zeenab ʕandik sandwitshaat 'eeh, min faDlik?
Girl ʕandi fuul wi Taʕmiyya w beeD wi kufta w kibda.
zeenab ʕandik gibna?
Girl la', maʕandiish gibna.
zeenab waaHid Taʕmiyya min faDlik.
Girl HaaDir.

8 ... and what soup they have.

Taari' misaa' ilkheer.
Waiter misaa' innuur.
Taari' fiih shurba?
Waiter 'aywa, y afandim. fiih shurba.
Taari' shurbit 'eeh?
Waiter fiih shurbit khuDaar, shurbit baSal.
Taari' iddiini shurbit baSal, min faDlak.
Waiter HaaDir.

9 Ordering a complete meal.

kamaal misaa' ilkheer.
Waiter misaa' innuur, ahlan wa sahlan.
kamaal shukran. ilminyu min faDlak.
Waiter itfaDDal. itfaDDali ya madaam.
huda/kamaal shukran.
huda min faDlak, ʕawza waaHid samak mashwi, wi waaHid baTaaTis, wi waaHid sabaanikh.
kamaal ʕaawiz waaHid ruzz wi waaHid firaakh wi waaHid bisilla, min faDlak.
Waiter Haaga kamaan?
kamaal 'aywa, itneen mayya maʕdaniyya min faDlak.
Waiter HaaDir.

Later

kamaal ilHisaab min faDlak.
Waiter itfaDDal.
kamaal itfaDDal ... da ʕalashaanak.
Waiter shukran. maʕa ssalaama.

Vocabulary

waaHid *one*
itneen *two*
talaata *three*
arba9a *four*
khamsa *five*
burTu'aan *orange*
gawaafa *guava*
manga *mango*
farawla *strawberry*
lamuun *lemon*
grepfruut *grapefruit*
minyu *menu*
sandwitsh *sandwich*
shurba *soup*
samak *fish*
firaakh *chicken*
mashwi *grilled*
ruzz *rice*
khuDaar *vegetables*
baTaaTis *potatoes*
bisilla *peas*
beeD *eggs*
fuul *cooked beans*
falaafil; ta٤miyya *deep-fried cakes of chick peas or beans*
kufta *meat balls*
kibda *liver*
gibna *cheese*
baSal *onion*
٤aSiir *juice*
mayya (ma٤daniyya) *(mineral) water*
biira *beer*
'ahwa *coffee*
shaay *tea*
shiisha *hubble bubble*
Haaga *thing, something*
Haaga sa'٤a *something cold*
maZbuuT *medium sweet*
ashrab *I drink*
tishrab *you* (m) *drink*
tishrabi *you* (f) *drink*
٤andak? *do you* (m) *have?*
mafiish *there isn't/aren't*
ma٤andiish *I haven't*
ya beeh *sir*
y afandim *sir*
ya madaam *madam*
... walla ... *... or ...*
ayyi khidma *can I help you?/don't mention it* (lit *any service*)
HaaDir *certainly, at once*
itfaDDal *here you* (m) *are*
itfaDDali *here you* (f) *are*
da ٤alashaanak *that's for you (when tipping a man)*

Explanations

- 'Have'

is expressed not by a verb but by means of **٤and-** (with), plus a personal ending, 'me', 'you' etc:

I have	٤and**i**
you have	٤and**ak** *(m)* ٤and**ik** *(f)*

eg **ع andak 'eeh?** what have you (*m*) got?
ع andak biira? do you have (any) beer?

- The same endings can be added to **ع alashaan** (for):
da ع alashaan**ak** 'that's for *you*' (*eg when giving a tip*). To a woman: da ع alashaan**ik**

- 'There is/are...' is the invariable **fiih**:

fiih ع aSiir?	is there (any) juice?
fiih biira?	is there (any) beer?
'aywa, fiih	yes, there is

- 'Not'

Both **fiih** and **ع and-** are made negative by adding **ma.....sh**:
ع andi I have; **maع andiish** I haven't
fiih there is; **mafiish** there isn't
mafiish biira hina there's no beer here

- 'I want' is:

ana ع aawiz (or **ع aayiz**) (if you're a man)
ana ع awza (or **ع ayza**) (if you're a woman)
ع aawiz is an adjective and so takes the feminine **-a** ending:
eg **hiyya ع awza ع aSiir** she wants (some) juice

ashrab	I drink
tishrab	you *(m)* drink
tishrabi	you *(f)* drink

When inviting someone to have a drink, say **tishrab 'eeh?** (to a man) or **tishrabi 'eeh?** (to a woman).

- You often add **-i** for the feminine:

itfaDDal, itfaDDali (*lit* kindly accept...)
This is used in any situation where you are offering something politely to somebody. It can

mean 'have a seat', 'please come in', 'have a drink', 'please join us' and so on.

- Noun + noun

  As in English, two nouns can come together, one modifying the other: eg **ʕaSiir lamuun** (lemon juice), **mudiir bank** (bank manager). But notice the order is reversed in Arabic. If the first noun ends in the feminine **-a,** this ending changes to **-it** when another noun follows:
  shurba soup, *but* **shurbit baSal** onion soup
  shurbit 'eeh? what soup?

- More than one

  A common way of forming the plural is by adding **-aat**, as in **sandwitsh, sandwitshaat.** The numbers from one to five are given in the vocabulary on page 25; when ordering food and drink, a number is used with the singular noun:
  itneen biira two beers
  itneen 'ahwa two coffees

- 'The'

  Put **il**- before the noun:
  Hisaab a bill; **ilHisaab** the bill
  The 'l' of **il** in some cases forms a long consonant with the following sound: **issabaanikh** - the spinach' (*not* ilsabaanikh). (See Guide to pronunciation, p11).

- Polite terms of address vary from country to country. In Egypt, some of the commonest, to a man, are **ya beeh** and **y afandim**; to a woman, **ya madaam.**

- If you are inviting someone to make a choice, the equivalent of '...or...?' is **...walla...?:**
  'ahwa walla shaay? coffee or tea?

Worth knowing

Besides eating in restaurants and hotels, you may want to eat at a snack bar, where you'll find sandwiches, often made with flat pitta-type bread (**khubz baladi**, or 'local bread') fried snacks like falaafil, kebab, and fresh fruit juice.
Fast food eating places are increasingly popular in the Middle East, and range from traditional roadside kiosks to the modern international food chains.

In some cake shops you can eat a delicious pastry on the spot with a glass of iced water, or take it with you.

Street cafes are for sipping tea, coffee and soft drinks at your leisure; in areas not much visited by tourists they tend to be patronised mainly by men. There the **shiisha** - the water pipe or 'hubble bubble' - is a common sight.

Islam forbids the consumption of alcohol and pork. Animals are slaughtered according to Islamic law, and the meat is then described as **Halaal** (literally 'permitted'). Official attitudes to alcohol vary a good deal from country to country, so it's best to check before taking any alcohol with you.

Ramadan is the month when Moslems fast during the hours of daylight, so it is generally polite not to eat, drink or smoke in public places during these hours.

If you order tea or coffee in a cafe, it will usually be served black - the tea with lots of sugar. Traditional 'Turkish' coffee can be **maZbuuT** (medium sweet), **saada** (without sugar) or **sukkar ziyaada** (very sweet).

Additional vocabulary

'akl *food*
sukkar *sugar*
laban *milk*
|Haliib *milk*|
malH *salt*
filfil *pepper*
talg *ice*
khubz *bread*
mezza *hors d'oeuvres*
Hummus *chick peas (often served as a creamy dip)*
TiHiina *sesame seed paste*
sálaTa khaDra *mixed salad*
makaroona *macaroni (or other pasta)*
bidingaan *aubergines*
faSulya *butter beans*
TamaaTim *tomatoes*
gambari *prawns, shrimps*
laHm *meat*
Hamaam *pigeon*
*|dajaaj *chicken*|
gazar *carrots*
shawirma *spiced grilled meat*
nibiit *wine*
'izaaza *bottle*
aHmar *red*
abyaD *white*
aiskriim *ice-cream*
mooz *bananas*
tuffaaH *apples*
mishmish *apricots*
tiin *figs*

Traditional oriental pastries often made with honey and nuts include **ba'laawa, basbuusa, kunaafa,** and **'aTaayif** - all of which may be served **b il'ishTa** - with whipped cream.

* Words shown in square brackets are not Egyptian but are in common use in other parts of the Arab World.

Exercises

1 Ask a waiter politely (ie say 'please') for the following:

a an orange juice
b two beers
c a sandwich

d a medium sweet coffee
e vegetable soup
f the bill

2 What would change if it were a waitress?

3 Ask whether the following are available, using **fiih**:

a coffee
b mango juice
c onion soup
d rice
e sandwiches

4 Ask for the same items using ع**andak.**

5 Think of questions or comments which might have prompted the following replies:

a 'aywa, عandi sandwitshaat gibna.
b la', mafiish nibiit hina.
c la', maعandiish mayya maعdaniyya.
d HaaDir....itfaDDal ilHisaab.
e عafwan.

Using the additional vocabulary at the end of the chapter try ordering a really elaborate meal!

3 Shopping

Key expressions

bi kam?	how much?
i<u>shsh</u>anTa di	this/that bag
ilgamal da	this/that camel
(bi) ع<u>ish</u>riin gineeh	(for) twenty pounds
mumkin	possible
mi<u>sh</u> mumkin	not possible
mumkin a<u>sh</u>tiri?	can I buy?
mumkin a<u>sh</u>uufha?	can I see it *(f)*?
di'ii'a waHda	one moment
(ana) 'aasif	(I'm) sorry *(m)*
(ana) 'asfa	(I'm) sorry *(f)*
عandak Sanf 'aHsan?	have you got a better kind?
عandak ma'aas 'akbar?	have you got a bigger size?
<u>gh</u>aali 'awi	very expensive
bi balaa<u>sh</u>	free (*lit* for nothing)

Conversations

1 Asking the price of a souvenir camel ...

Taari' min faDlak, bi kam ilgamal da?
Shopkeeper b itneen gineeh wi nuSS.
Taari' bi kam?
Shopkeeper itneen gineeh wi nuSS.
Taari' w ilkibiir?
Shopkeeper <u>kh</u>amsa gineeh.
Taari' <u>sh</u>ukran.
Shopkeeper ilعafw.

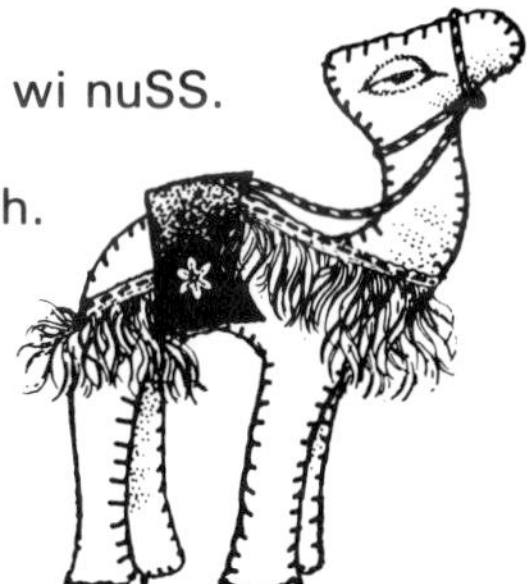

2 ... a bag ...

Taari'	SabaaH ilkheer.
Shopkeeper	SabaaH innuur.
Taari'	bi kam ishshanTa di?
Shopkeeper	ƹishriin gineeh.
Taari'	wi di?
Shopkeeper	itnaashar gineeh.
Taari'	bi kam?
Shopkeeper	itnaashar gineeh.
Taari'	shukran.
Shopkeeper	ƹafwan.

3 ... and a galabiyya.

Taari'	bi kam ilgallabiyya di?
Shopkeeper	sabƹa gineeh wi nuSS.
Taari'	w ilHamra di?
Shopkeeper	w ilHamra di, bi tamanya gineeh.
Taari'	shukran.
Shopkeeper	ayy*i* khidma.

4 zeenab wants some postcards.

zeenab	ƹandak kart buSTaal, min faDlak?
Shopkeeper	'aywa, ƹandi. itfaDDali.
zeenab	bi kam ilkart?
Shopkeeper	bi ƹashar 'uruush.

zeenab	*(she chooses three)* talaata min faDlak.
Shopkeeper	talatiin 'irsh, min faDlik.
zeenab	ʿandak Tawaabiʿ, min faDlak?
Shopkeeper	la', 'aasif, maʿandiish.
zeenab	shukran ... itfaDDal gineeh.
Shopkeeper	itfaDDali khamsiin, sittiin, sabʿiin.
zeenab	shukran.
Shopkeeper	maʿa ssalaama.
zeenab	maʿa ssalaama.

5 Can I buy stamps here?

Taari'	mumkin ashtiri Tawaabiʿ hina?
Shopgirl	'aywa, mumkin.
Taari'	iddiini talat Tawaabiʿ l ingiltira, min faDlik.
Shopgirl	HaaDir.

6 A film for the camera.

Taari'	mumkin ashtiri film l ilkamera di?
Shopgirl	mumkin ashuufha?
Taari'	*(handing it over)* itfaDDali.
Shopgirl	sitta w talatiin, walla arbaʿa w ʿishriin Suura?
Taari'	sitta w talatiin mulawwan.
Shopgirl	HaaDir. di'ii'a waHda. *(she fetches a film)* itfaDDal. talaata gineeh wi khamsa w sabʿiin 'irsh.
Taari'	itfaDDali.
Shopgirl	shukran.
Taari'	shukran. maʿa ssalaama.
Shopgirl	maʿa ssalaama.

7 Sometimes you'll have to bargain ...

Customer	issalaamu ʿaleekum.
Shopkeeper	ʿaleekum issalaam.
Customer	min faDlak, bi kam ishshanTa di?
Shopkeeper	bi tamanya w ʿishriin gineeh.
Customer	la', mish mumkin. ghalya 'awi.

Shopkeeper	bi balaash ᶜalashaanik ... ᶜawzaaha bi kam?
Customer	bi ᶜishriin gineeh.
Shopkeeper	la'! mumkin bi talaata w ᶜishriin.
Customer	Tayyib. itfaDDal.
Shopkeeper	shukran. maᶜa ssalaama.

8 ... or ask for a better kind ...

Customer	ᶜandak Sanf 'aHsan?
Shopkeeper	'aywa, ᶜandi. bass ghaali.
Customer	ᶜandak Sanf 'aHsan?
Shopkeeper	la'. da 'aHsan Sanf.

9 ... or a larger size ...

Customer	ᶜandak ma'aas 'akbar?
Shopkeeper	ᶜandi. ma'aas kam?
Customer	itneen w arbiᶜiin.

10 ... or something cheaper.

Customer	fiih Haaga 'arkhaS?
Shopgirl	la', 'asfa, mafiish.

Vocabulary

bi *for* (in prices), *with*
gallabiyya (*pl* -aat) *galabiyya*
gineeh *pound*
'irsh (*pl* 'uruush) *piastre*
kart (*pl* kuruut) buSTaal *postcard*
Taabiᶜ (*pl* Tawaabiᶜ) *stamp*
nuSS *half*
'aHmar (*f* Hamra) *red*
kámera *camera*
film (*pl* aflaam) *film*
mulawwan *coloured, in colour*
di'ii'a *minute, moment*
Suura (*pl* Suwar) *picture*
ghaali (*f* ghalya) *expensive*
li *to, for*
'awi *very, too*
ashtiri *I buy*
bass *but, only*
'aHsan *better, best*
rikhiiS *cheap*
'arkhaS *cheaper, cheapest*
kibiir *big*
'akbar *bigger, biggest*
Sanf (*pl* 'aSnaaf) *kind, type*
ma'aas *size*
Tayyib ... *OK, well now ...*

Numbers

6 sitta (*before plural noun* - sitt)
7 sabƐa (*before plural noun* - sabaƐ)
8 tamanya (*before plural noun* - taman)
9 tisƐa (*before plural noun* - tisaƐ)
10 Ɛáshara (*before plural noun* - Ɛashar)

11	Hidaashar	16	sittaashar
12	itnaashar	17	sabaƐtaashar
13	talattaashar	18	tamantaashar
14	arbaƐtaashar	19	tisaƐtaashar
15	khamastaashar		

20	Ɛishriin	50	khamsiin	80	tamaniin
30	talatiin	60	sittiin	90	tisƐiin
40	arbiƐiin	70	sabƐiin	100	miyya

NB As with 6-10 above, talaata becomes talat and arbaƐa, arbaƐ before a plural noun.

Explanations

- To ask the price of an object:

bi kam	**ilgallabiyya?**	how much is	the galabiyya?
	ilgamal?		the camel?
	ishshanTa?		the bag?

or: **ilgallabiyya bi kam?**

The answer will be:

(bi)	gineeh	£1	
	itneen gineeh	£2	
	khamsa gineeh	£5	and so on

- **kam?** alone is used before a noun to mean 'how many?' or 'how much?', referring to quantities. The noun is always *singular:*

kam kart?	how many cards?
kam sandwitsh?	how many sandwiches?
kam sukkar?	how much sugar?

- Adjectives have to add an -**a** to agree with feminine pronouns:
ana/inta/huwwa kwayyis

ana/inti/hiyya kwayyisa
They also agree with feminine nouns.

ilgamal *(m)*	the camel
ilgamal kibiir	the camel is big
ishshanTa *(f)*	the bag
ishshanTa kibiira	the bag is big

Not all adjectives make the feminine like **kwayyisa**. We show other types like this:

'aHmar (*f* Hamra)	*red*
ghaali (*f* ghalya)	*expensive*

- To say 'a big bag' or 'an expensive galabiyya':
  shanTa kibiira
  gallabiyya ghalya

- To say 'the big bag' or 'the expensive galabiyya', add **il-** to the adjective as well as the noun but remember the rules given on p11:
  ishshanTa ilkibiira
  ilgallabiyya ilghalya

- 'This' or 'that'
  Make the noun definite (by putting **il-** first), then add **da** to a masculine, **di** to a feminine noun:

ilgamal da	this/that camel
ilgallabiyya di	this/that galabiyya

If it's clear what you're talking about, **da** or **di** can be used alone. So can any adjective:

da bi kam?	how much is that *(m)*?
di ghalya!	that *(f)* is expensive!
w ilkibiir	and the big one *(m)*?
w ilHamra?	and the red one *(f)*?

- To make a 'verbless' statement negative, add mish as follows:

ana min landan	**ana mish min landan**
huwwa hina	**huwwa mish hina**
da ghaali	**da mish ghaali**

- One way of forming plurals is to add -**aat** (see p27):
  sandwitsh   **sandwitshaat**

  Often nothing is added, but the pattern of vowels in the word is rearranged (a bit like English 'mouse, mice').
  kart (a card)   **kuruut** (cards)
  'irsh (a piastre)   **'uruush** (piastres)
  The pattern used for **Taabiع** (a stamp) is **Tawaabiع.**

  There are about half a dozen major patterns (see Reference section p71-72). You can't necessarily predict the plural, so we give the main ones in the vocabulary lists like this:
  film (*pl* aflaam)

- The numbers 1 - 5 were given on p25; 6 - 100 are given on p35.

  waaHid (one) has the feminine form **waHda.** eg
  di'ii'a waHda one moment

  To say '24', '35', etc, Arabic uses 'four and twenty', 'five and thirty' etc:
  arbaعa w عishriin: 24   **khamsa w talatiin**: 35

  It's useful to divide the numbers into two sets: up to ten, and eleven upwards.
  The numbers 2 - 10 are followed by a plural noun (*except* when ordering food and drink), and the final -**a** of the number is dropped:
  talaata (on its own), *but*
  talat Tawaabiع   three stamps
  عashar 'uruush   ten piastres

  Numbers from eleven upwards don't change and are followed by a *singular* noun:
  talatiin 'irsh   thirty piastres
  arbaعa w عishriin Suura   twenty-four pictures

- Basic units of length and weight are invariable:

  mitr   a metre
  khamsa mitr   five metres

kiilu a kilo
sitta kiilu six kilos

The same applies to **gineeh** (the Egyptian £):
gineeh £1
talaata gineeh £3

- To say 'three and a half pounds' (*or* kilos *etc*) add **wi nuSS** after the noun:
talaata gineeh wi nuSS; khamsa kiilu wi nuSS etc

- To say 'a kilo of ...':

kiilu ilburTu'aan	a kilo of oranges
nuSS kiilu issamak	half a kilo of fish
khamsa kiilu ilbaTaaTis	five kilos of potatoes

- **mumkin?** on its own means 'is it possible?', 'can I?', 'may I?', 'can we?', etc. The answer will be:
'aywa, mumkin *or*
la', mish mumkin

- To say 'I buy' and 'I see':

(ana)	**ashtiri**	I buy
	ashuuf	I see

Add **mumkin** (is it possible?) to ask 'can I ...?':

mumkin	**ashtiri?**	can I buy?
	ashuuf?	can I see?

- **-ha** ('it' for feminine nouns) or **-u** (for masculine nouns) may be added to the end:
mumkin ashuufha? can I see it? (*eg* ilkámera)
mumkin ashuufu? can I see it? (*eg* ilgamal)

NB In conversation 7, the shopkeeper says **ذawzaaha bi kam?** (how much do you want to pay? - *lit* you want it for how much?) referring to **ishshanTa**.

- Good, better, best ...

A special pattern is used for the comparative

and superlative of adjectives:

kibiir (big)	**'akbar** (bigger, biggest)
rikhiiS (cheap)	**'arkhaS** (cheaper, cheapest)
kitiir (a lot)	**'aktar** (more, most) etc

kwayyis (good) has the special comparative **'aHsan** (better, best). So:

iSSanf da kwayyis	this kind is good
iSSanf da 'aHsan	that kind is better

The comparative *follows* the noun:

fiih Sanf 'aHsan? is there a better kind?

The superlative *precedes* it:

da 'aHsan Sanf that's the best kind

Fortunately these comparatives don't change in the feminine!

Additional vocabulary

fluus *money*
shibshib *slippers*
sandal (*pl* sanaadil) *sandal*
'amiiS (*pl* 'umSaan) *shirt*
fustaan (*pl* fasatiin) *dress*
'umaash *material*
'uTn *cotton*
Hariir *silk*
gild *leather*
'ufTaan (*pl* 'afaTiin) *kaftan*
banTaloon *trousers*
gazma (*pl* gizam) *shoe*
kanaka *coffee pot*
sanduu' *box*
'alam *pen, pencil*
Hilw *beautiful, fine*
sigaara (*pl* sagaayir) *cigarette*
kibriit *matches*
raTl *pound, half a kilo*
Sughayyar *small*
'aSghar *smaller, smallest*

Worth knowing

Currencies Besides the Egyptian gineeh, other currencies to be found in the Arab World are the riyaal, the dinaar, the liira and the dirham.

Bargaining

This is the accepted practice in the Middle East, at least when it comes to buying souvenirs. It is an amiable and often leisurely process - pursued over coffee or tea if a large item like a carpet is involved - but no offence is taken if you decide to 'think it over'. In countries where taxis don't have meters (or the meters tend not to work!), it's just as well to fix the price before you get in.

The galabiyya - a loose cotton gown ideal for hot climates - is the traditional form of dress for men in most Arab countries. It is usually simple in design -plain or striped - though more elaborate and brilliantly-coloured galabiyyas are produced for tourists. In Egypt, businessmen and office workers will probably wear European clothes rather than the galabiyya. In many other Arab countries though, it is the most usual form of dress for men of all classes.

The kaftan, a more formal version of the galabiyya, is often a heavier silk/cotton mixture - or wool for the winter - and is worn by both men and women.

Exercises

1 What is the difference in meaning between these four sentences?

a shanTa kibiira
b ishshanTa ilkibiira
c ishshanTa kibiira
d ishshanTa di kibiira

2 Ask a shopkeeper 'Have you got..., please?':

a any postcards
b any stamps
c a colour film
d a large bag
e a red galabiyya

3 Ask him if you can see the following:

a a galabiyya
b that camera
c a larger size
d a cheaper kind

4 Ask a shopkeeper the price of the following (checking your vocabulary from Chapter 2):

a a kilo of oranges
b half a kilo of lemons
c two kilos of bananas
d half a kilo of sugar

5 A shopkeeper gives the price of various items: tell him 'That is very expensive', using **da** or **di** as appropriate.

a ilgallabiyya bi talatiin gineeh.
b ilkart bi sittiin 'irsh.
c mitr il'umaash bi khamsa gineeh.
d ishshanTa bi itneen wi Ɛishriin gineeh.

6 Ask him if there is:
a a bigger bag
b a smaller dress
c a cheaper camera
d a better kind

4 In the hotel

Key expressions

عandak 'ooDa?	do you have a room?
fiih mayya sukhna?	is there hot water?
عandi Hagz	I've got a reservation
kam leela?	how many nights?
bi kam illeela?	how much a night?
30 gineeh f ilyoom	£30 a day
'ooDa nimra ...	room number ...
issaaعa kam?	what time is it?/at what time?
issaaعa sabعa	(it's) seven o'clock
mumkin adfaع ilHisaab?	can I pay the bill?
mumkin aعmil tilifoon?	can I make a phone call?
mumkin aghayyar dolaraat?	can I change some dollars?
عala lyimiin/shshimaal	on the right/the left
imDi hina	sign here

Conversations

1 Taari' is booking a hotel room.

Taari'	misaa' ilkheer.
Clerk	misaa' innuur.
Taari'	عandak 'ooDa, min faDlak?
Clerk	di'ii'a waHda. *(checks in register)* 'aywa fiih. kam leela?
Taari'	leela waHda. fiih mayya sukhna?
Clerk	'aywa, wi fiih banyu wi tilifoon wi tilivizyoon f il'ooDa.
Taari'	bi kam il'ooDa?
Clerk	talatiin gineeh f ilyoom.
Taari'	iddiini 'ooDa, min faDlak.
Clerk	HaaDir.

2 zeenab wants a room for two nights.

zeenab	ɛandak 'ooDa, min faDlak?
Clerk	di'ii'a waHda. *(looks in register)* kam leela?
zeenab	lelteen, min faDlak.
Clerk	'aywa fiih.
zeenab	ɛayza 'ooDa bi Hammaam.
Clerk	fiih, mawguud.
zeenab	bi kam?
Clerk	tamanya w arbiɛiin gineeh.
zeenab	fiih maTɛam hina?
Clerk	'aywa, fiih maTɛam *(pointing)* hinaak.
zeenab	ilfiTaar issaaɛa kam?
Clerk	min sabɛa l ɛáshara.

3 If you already have a reservation ...

Taari'	ana ɛandi Hagz hina, min faDlak?.
Clerk	ismak 'eeh?
Taari'	Taari' ilbaguuri.
Clerk	'aywa, maZbuuT.
Taari'	shukran.
Clerk	da ilmuftaaH. il'ooDa suttumiyya w waaHid. il'asanSiir 'uddaam ɛala lyimiin.
Taari'	shukran. ilfiTaar issaaɛa kam?
Clerk	ilfiTaar min issaaɛa sabɛa l issaaɛa ɛáshara, hinaak f ilmaTɛam.
Taari'	shukran.
Clerk	ilɛafw.

4 Asking for the bill.

Taari'	mumkin adfaɛ ilHisaab, min faDlak?
Clerk	mumkin. di'ii'a waHda.
Taari'	shukran.

5 You may not always be lucky ...

Man	SabaaH ilkheer.
Clerk	SabaaH innuur.

Man	min faDlak, fiih 'ooDa faDya?
Clerk	ʕandak Hagz?
Man	la', maʕandiish.
Clerk	'aasif, il'utiil malyaan.

6 And you may have to sign the register ...

Clerk	imDi hina min faDlak. iktib ismak w ism baladak.
Man	bi kulli suruur.
Clerk	itfaDDal ilmuftaaH. 'ooDa nimra miteen wi talatiin, f iddoor ittaani.
Man	shukran.

7 Can I call London?

Man	mumkin akallim landan min hina?
Clerk	mumkin. ittilifoon hina ʕala shshimaal.
Man	shukran.

8 Changing money.

Man	mumkin aghayyar miyya w khamsiin dolaar?
Clerk	'aywa, Tabʕan. ilbasbuur, min faDlak.
Man	mumkin aghayyar shikaat siyaHiyya kamaan?
Clerk	'aywa, dolaraat kamaan?
Man	la', istirliini.

9 Making a phone call.

Man	mumkin aʕmil tilifoon min hina?
Clerk	bi kulli suruur.
Man	*(dials)* ... 'alo? ... 'aywa, ya maHmuud! izzayyak inta? ... ilHamdu lillaah ... ana fi 'utiil shahriZaad, 'ooDa nimra miteen wi talatiin...Tayyib, bukra in sha'allaa h. tiSbaH ʕala kheer.

Vocabulary

'ooDa (*pl* 'owaD) *room*
leela (*pl* layaali) *night*
sukhna *hot*
banyu *bath*
tilifoon *telephone*
tilivizyoon *television*
yoom (*pl* 'ayyaam) *day*
Hammaam *bathroom*
mawguud *there is*
maTعam (*pl* maTaaعim) *restaurant*
hinaak *there*
fiTaar *breakfast*
saaعa *hour, time*
Hagz *reservation*
maZbuuT *right, exact*
muftaaH *key*
'asanSiir *lift*
'uddaam *opposite, in front*
عala *on*
yimiin *right*
shimaal *left*
adfaع *I pay*
faaDi (*f* faDya) *empty, free*
malyaan *full*
iktib *write*
imDi *sign*
balad *town, country*
nimra *number*
door *floor*
taani (*f* tanya) *second*
akallim *I speak to*
aghayyar *I change*
dolaar (*pl dolaraat) dollar*
Tabعan *of course*
basbuur *passport*
shiik (*pl* -aat) siyaHiyya *travellers cheque*
istirliini *sterling*
aعmil tilifoon *I make a phone call*
bi kull*i* suruur *certainly* (lit *with all pleasure)*
tiSbaH(i) عala kheer *good night*
siriir *bed*
'aakul *I eat*
dushsh *shower*

Explanations

- To ask for a room:
  عandak 'ooDa?

  To specify:

'ooDa bi	**Hammaam**	bathroom
	dushsh	shower
	mayya sukhna	hot water
	sirireen	two beds

  To say you've got a reservation:
  (ana) عandi Hagz

  You'll be told the price per day:

عishriin talatiin	**gineeh f ilyoom**

- One ...

  waaHid *(m)* **waHda** *(f)*
  eg **yoom waaHid** **leela waHda**

- Two ...

  itneen gineeh £2
  itneen biira two beers
  But most nouns have a special 'dual' form in which -**een** is added to the singular:
  yoom day **yomeen** two days
  siriir bed **sirireen** two beds
  If the noun is feminine, drop the -**a** and add -**teen:**
  leela night **lelteen** two nights
  di'ii'a moment **di'i'teen** two moments
  The dual of 'hundred' (**miyya**) is **miteen.**

- Hundreds

  On p76 of the reference section, you will find the forms taken by numbers 3 - 9 when they precede 'hundred'. In the hotel (conversation 3) the clerk says **suttumiyya** (six hundred).

- To ask the time:

  issaaꜥa kam? (*lit* the hour how much?) has two meanings: 'what time is it?' and 'at what time?'
  To ask 'what time is ...?':
  ilfiTaar **issaaꜥa kam?** what time is breakfast?

- To tell the time:

issaaꜥa	talaata	(it's)	three o'clock
	khamsa		five o'clock
	sitta w nuSS		half past six

  To say 'from ... to ...':
  min issaaꜥa sabꜥa **l** issaaꜥa ꜥashara

- Directions

(ish)shimaal (the) left
(il)yimiin (the) right

They often come after ع**ala** ('on'):

ع**ala** | **lyimiin** / **shshimaal**

- **'uddaam** (in front, opposite)

It can be used on its own or take one of the pronouns:

'uddaamak in front of you *(m)*
'uddaamik in front of you *(f)*
'uddaamha in front of her

- Verbs

More examples of 'I ...'

(ana)	**adfa**ع	pay
	aakul	eat
	aghayyar	change
	aع**mil**	make, do
	akallim	call (*lit* speak to)

The above are all in the first person (I) and so all begin with **a**-. To make the second person (you), change the **a**- to **ti**-:

tishrab 'eeh? what are you drinking?
mumkin **tidfa**ع**?** can you pay?
mumkin **tighayyar?** can you change?

NB mumkin **taakul** hina you can eat here

These are used when talking to a man. If talking to a woman, add a final -**i**:

tishrabi 'eeh?
mumkin **tidfa**ع**i?**
mumkin **tighayyari?**

NB mumkin **takli** hina

To tell someone to do something (the 'imperative'), the initial **t**- is dropped:

iktib (ismak) write (your name) *(to a man)*
iktibi (ismik) write (your name) *(to a woman)*

iddiini (give me) is another imperative of this kind.

- Polite phrases

Apart from the phrases you are now familiar with, like **min faDlak** (please), **shukran** (thank you) and so on, you will also hear **bi kulli suruur** (certainly) - an even politer version of **HaaDir**!

In conversation 9, Taari' says **tiSbaH ʿala kheer** (good night), which shows he's speaking to a man. To a woman, he'd have said **tiSbaHi ʿala kheer**. It literally means 'may the morning find you well'.

Additional vocabulary

[ghurfa *room*]
[gawaaz issafar *passport*]
fuuTa (*pl* fuwaT) *towel*
niDiif *clean*
wisikh *dirty*
haadi *quiet*
dawsha *noise*
ʿaTlaan *out of order, not working*
ittilifoon ʿaTlaan *the phone's not working*
shaghghaal *working*
mish shaghghaal *not working*
b ilfiTaar *including breakfast*
il'ooDa b ilfiTaar *bed and breakfast*
istiqbaal *reception*
doorit mayya *lavatory*
twalett *lavatory*
takyiif hawa *air conditioning*
khidma *service*
ʿáshara f ilmiyya *10%*

Worth knowing

Information on accommodation, including up-to-date lists of hotels of various categories, can usually be obtained from the National Tourist Office of the country you are going to visit. This may not include much on the cheaper end of the market; if you want to live really simply, ask around on your arrival. Taxi drivers in the Middle East, as elsewhere, are usually invaluable sources of information.

Exercises

1 You are booking into a hotel; check whether there is:

a a bathroom
b a shower
c a telephone
d hot water

2 Now complain that the first three are not working (**ʕaTlaan**) and there's no hot water!

3 Ask whether you can:

a pay the bill
b make a phone call
c change some dollars

4 You want a single room for two nights; fill in your part of the conversation that follows, remembering to ask how much it costs!

Clerk	SabaaH ilkheer.
You	...
Clerk	ayy*i* khidma?
You	...
Clerk	'aywa, fiih. bi siriir waaHid walla bi sirireen?
You	...
Clerk	kam leela?
You	...
Clerk	fiih 'ooDa Hilwa f iddoor ittaani. itfaDDal ilmuftaaH.
You	...
Clerk	ʕishriin gineeh bass.

5 Out and about

Key expressions

il'utiil feen? **feen il'utiil?**	where is the hotel?
'awwil / taani shaariع	first / second street
'urayyib (min hina)	near (here)
bi9iid (min hina)	far (from here)
laazim taakhud taksi	you (m) must take a taxi
عaawiz aruuH ilharam	I want to go to the pyramids
shuwayya	a little, quite
kitiir	a lot
tazkara l iskindriyya	a ticket to Alexandria
dáraga 'uula / tanya	first / second class
raayiH/raayiH gayy	single/return
raSiif nimra kam?	which platform?
feen 'a'rab 'agzakhaana?	where's the nearest chemist's?
imshi عala Tool	go straight on
da 'aTr iskindriyya?	is this the Alexandria train?

Conversations

1 Asking for a free map of the town.

Taari'	min faDlak?
Clerk	'aywa?
Taari'	عandak khariiTa l ilqaahira?
Clerk	'aywa.
Taari'	mumkin aakhud waHda?
Clerk	itfaDDal.
Taari'	shukran.
Clerk	عafwan.

2 Asking your way to Liberation Square.

Taari'	min faDlik, feen midaan ittaHriir?
Passerby	'awwil shaari**ع** ... *(correcting herself)* la', taani shaari**ع** **ع**ala lyimiin.
Taari'	shukran.
Passerby	**ع**afwan.

3 Is Khan El Khalili nearby?

Taari'	min faDlak, khan ilkhaliili 'urayyib min hina?
Passerby	la', bi**ع**iid shuwayya. laazim taakhud taksi.
Taari'	shukran.
Passerby	**ع**afwan.

4 Where is the nearest chemist's?

Tourist	min faDlak, feen 'a'rab 'agzakhaana?
Passerby	'awwil shaari**ع** **ع**ala shshimaal.
Tourist	shukran.

5 Calling a taxi ...

mu'nis	taksi! taksi! **ع**aawiz aruuH ilharam.
Driver	bi khamsa gineeh.
mu'nis	khamsa gineeh? kitiir! arba**ع**a?
Driver	mumkin. itfaDDal.
mu'nis	shukran

6 ... and directing the taxi driver.

Driver	feen il'utiil?
mu'nis	imshi **ع**ala Tool ...
Driver	*(drives on)* wi dilwa'ti?
mu'nis	shimaal hina ...
Driver	shimaal feen? shimaal hina?
mu'nis	'aywa. wi ba**ع**deen taani shaari**ع** **ع**ala lyimin.
Driver	hina?
mu'nis	'aywa. shukran.
Driver	il**ع**afw.

7 Finding out about planes to Aswan.

Taari misaa' ilkheer.
Assistant misaa' innuur.
Taari' ana عaayiz aruuH 'aSwaan.
Assistant imta?
Taari' baعd bukra.
Assistant baعd bukra? litneen.
Taari' 'aywa.
Assistant di'ii'a waHda. *(looking in timetable)* fiih Tayyaara issaaعa tamanya wi khamsa w arbiعiin iSSubH, wi Tayyaara issaa9a itnaashar wi nuSS iDDuhr.
Taari' shukran. bi kam ittazkara?
Assistant raayiH walla raayiH gayy?
Taari' raayiH gayy.
Assistant raayiH gayy? sabعa w arbiعiin gineeh.

8 Buying a train ticket.

Taari' tazkara l iskindriyya min faDlak.
Clerk dáraga 'uula walla dáraga tanya?
Taari' dáraga 'uula.
Clerk dáraga 'uula tamanha khamsa gineeh.
Taari' *(giving him the money)* itfaDDal. raSiif nimra kam?
Clerk raSiif nimra arbaعa.
Taari' shukran.
Clerk عafwan.

9 Checking that it's the right train.

Taari' min faDlak?
Passerby 'aywa?
Taari' da 'aTr iskindriyya?
Passerby 'aywa. da 'aTr iskindriyya.
Taari' shukran.
Passerby عafwan.

10 zeenab is going to the Egyptian museum in Cairo.

zeenab	min faDlak!
Passerby	'aywa?
zeenab	ilmatHaf feen?
Passerby	imshi ع ala Tool, wi taani shaariع ع ala lyimiin.
zeenab	shukran.
Passerby	ع afwan.

Later

zeenab	bi kam ittazkara, min faDlak?
Attendant	tazkara bi talaata gineeh.
zeenab	iddiini tazkarteen.
Attendant	itneen ... sitta gineeh.

Vocabulary

khariiTa (l ilqaahira) *map (of Cairo)*
midaan *square*
midaan ittaHriir *Liberation Square*
'awwil (*f* 'uula) *first*
shaariع (*pl* shawaariع) *street*
khan ilkhaliili *Khan El Khalili (bazaar area of Cairo)*
laazim *(it is) necessary*
taksi (*pl* taksiyyaat) *taxi*
'a'rab *nearest*
'agzakhaana *chemist's*
aruuH *I go*
haram *pyramids*
ع ala Tool *straight on*
dilwa'ti *now*
baعdeen *later, then*
baعd bukra *the day after tomorrow*
litneen *Monday*
Tayyaara (*pl* Tayyaraat) *aeroplane*
SubH *morning*
Duhr *noon*
baعd iDDuhr *afternoon*
tazkara (*pl* tazaakir) *ticket*
dáraga *class*
taman *price*
raSiif *platform*
'aTr *train*

Explanations

- To ask 'where is ...?':

  il'utiil **feen?** *or*
  feen il'utiil?

- Near or far

'urayyib (min)	near (to)
biᶜiid (min)	far (from)
da 'urayyib min hina?	is that near here?
da biᶜiid min il'utiil?	is that far from the hotel?

- Nearer and nearest

The key word is **'a'rab.**
'a'rab 'agzakhaana - the nearest chemist (adjective first), *but*
fiih 'agzakhaana 'a'rab min il'utiil? - is there a chemist nearer to the hotel? (adjective second).

- First and second

	m	*f*
1st	**'awwil**	**'uula**
2nd	**taani**	**tanya**

You'll hear the masculine versions when you're being told which street to take:

'awwil	**shaariᶜ**	**ᶜala lyimiin**	1st on the right
taani		**ᶜala shshimaal**	2nd on the left

and the feminine versions when you're asked if you want to travel 1st or 2nd class (notice that here they follow the noun):
dáraga 'uula walla dáraga tanya?

- The 'I' and 'you' forms of 'go' and 'take' are:

aakhud	I take	**aruuh**	I go
taakhud	you *(m)* take	**tiruuH**	you *(m) go*
takhdi	you *(f)* take	**tiruuHi**	you *(f)* go

Any of these forms can follow **mumkin:**
mumkin aakhud waHda? can I take one?
'aywa, mumkin taakhud waHda yes, you can take one

The imperatives of these are:
khud! *(to a man)* take!
khudi! *(to a woman)*

ruuH! *(to a man)* **ruuHi!** *(to a woman)*	go!

The other verb 'go' which you'll hear in street directions (meaning 'go on') is:

amshi	I go
timshi	you *(m and f)* go
imshi!	go! *(m and f)*
imshi ﻋala Tool!	go straight on!

- To say 'must':

use **laazim** (it is necessary), which is invariable and works like **mumkin** (see p38):

laazim taakhud taksi	you must take a taxi
laazim tiruuH il'utiil	you must go to the hotel

- **ﻋaawiz** and **ﻋawza** ('want') also work like **mumkin**, except that there are separate masculine and feminine forms:

I want to ...

ﻋaawiz **ﻋawza**	aﻋmil tilifoon aruuH 'aSwaan

You want to .../do you want to ...?

ﻋaawiz tishrab 'ahwa? *(to a man)*
ﻋawza tiruuHi ilharam? *(to a woman)*

- More times and dates

To talk about fractions of the hour, say **nuSS** (half), **rubﻋ** (quarter) and **tilt** (third, ie twenty minutes):

issaaﻋa talaata w nuSS	it's (*or* at) half past three
issaaﻋa tamanya w rubﻋ	it's (*or* at) quarter past eight
issaaﻋa itneen wi tilt	it's (*or* at) two twenty

If minutes are referred to, the ordinary numbers are used:

issaaﻋa waHda w ﻋáshara	ten past one

To say 'a quarter to ...' or 'ten to ...', use **illa** (less):
issaaعa arbaعa illa rubع   a quarter to four
issaaعa talaata illa عáshara/khamsa   ten/five to three

Days of the week are given on p74-75, together with the months.
yoom litneen (*lit* 'day two' of the Muslim week) is Monday. Often **yoom** is omitted: **litneen.**

Days of the month are simple: the appropriate number is used before the name of the month:
khamastaashar fibraayir (on) the 15th February
sitta mayyu   (on) the 6th May

- In chapter 3, a girl said **mumkin ashuufha?** (can I see it?), talking about the camera.
  In this chapter, at the station the ticket clerk says **tamanha khamsa gineeh** (*lit* its cost is £5). The feminine -**ha** shows he's talking about **tazkara** (ticket) - another feminine noun.

Additional vocabulary

muwaSalaat *transport*
maHaTTa *station, stop*
maHaTTit il'aTr *railway station*
'utubiis (*pl* 'utubisaat) *bus*
maHaTTit il'utubiis *bus stop*
عarabiyya *car*
[sayyaara, *pl* sayyaraat *car*]
b il'aTr *by train*
b il'utubiis *by bus*
b ilعarabiyya *by car*
sawwaa' *driver*
maTaar *airport*
asaafir *I travel, leave*
badri *early*
wakhri *late*
maftuuH *open*
ma'fuul *closed*
maktab ilbariid *post office*
maktab SiyaaHa *tourist office*
'ism buliis *police station*
mustashfa *hospital*
sifaara *embassy*
suu' *market, bazaar*

Worth knowing

Most towns and cities in the Middle East have a 'bazaar' area, part of which may specialise in tourist souvenirs, but where you will also find whole streets devoted to textiles, carpets, gold, jewellery, household goods, herbs and spices, and so on. Like Khan El Khalili in Cairo and the Hamidiyya bazaar in Damascus, they are often at the heart of the old city, by the walls of the earliest mosques and palaces. In North Africa the old part part of the city, the 'medina', is usually a maze of narrow lanes, surrounded by the original medieval walls.

Preferred modes of transport vary from country to country. The system of sharing taxis, especially between towns, is common; they generally operate between fixed points and you change to a 'local' taxi on your arrival. It's best to agree beforehand

on taxi fares, and to make it clear in advance if, for example, you want the driver to wait for you and then bring you back, with the words **mumkin tistanna hinaak, min faDlak?** (can you wait there, please?).

There is not a tradition of hitchhiking in the Middle East, and some countries actively discourage it. In any case, buses are extremely cheap and a very good way of meeting people.

The Egyptian Museum (**ilmatHaf ilmaSri**) in Cairo houses the world's most important collection of Egyptian antiquities dating back to the earliest civilisations. The collection includes monuments of the pharaohs, statues and jewellery, the treasure from the tomb of Tutankhamun and one of the great artistic masterpieces of all time - the gold mask of Tutankhamun.

Exercises

1 Tell someone 'I want ...':

a to take a taxi

b to go to the pyramids

c to go to the hotel
d to go to the museum
e a ticket to Aswan

2 Tell a man 'You must ...':
a take a taxi
b see the pyramids
c pay the bill
d go to the chemist's

3 Now say the same things to a woman.

4 Tell the taxi driver to:
a go straight on
b turn left
c take the first street on the right

5 You want to buy a first class return train ticket to Aswan. Fill in your part of the conversation.

Clerk	ayy*i* <u>kh</u>idma? ʿaawiz tiruuH feen?
You	...
Clerk	dáraga 'uula walla dáraga tanya?
You	...
Clerk	raayiH walla raayiH gayy?
You	...
Clerk	tazkara dáraga 'uula tamanha sitta gineeh.
You	...
Clerk	<u>sh</u>ukran.

6 What times are being given here?
a issaaʿa <u>kh</u>amsa w nuSS
b issaaʿa itneen wi rubʿ
c issaaʿa ʿá<u>sh</u>ara w tilt
d issaaʿa talaata illa <u>kh</u>amsa
e issaaʿa waHda illa rubʿ

6 Business and pleasure

Key expressions

ilmudiir mawguud?	is the manager in?
mish kida?	isn't it?/isn't that so?
batkallim ʿárabi	I speak Arabic
a'addimlak	let me introduce you to
furSa saʿiida	pleased to meet you (*lit* a happy occasion)
ʿandi maʿaad (maʿa)	I have an appointment (with)
kallimni	ring me
sharraftuuna	you have honoured us
nawwartu beetna	you have honoured us
mumkin awaSSalku?	can I give you *(pl)* a lift?
maʿa 'alf salaama	goodbye (*lit* with a thousand farewells)

Conversations

1 Making an appointment by phone.

Secretary	'alo?
kaamil	'alo? min faDlak, ilmudiir mawguud?
Secretary	'aywa, mawguud. issayyid kaamil, mish kida? di'ii'a waHda *(she puts him through).*
Director	'aywa ya sayyid kaamil. ayyi khidma?
kaamil	mumkin ashuufak baʿd bukra?
Director	ʿandi maʿaad iSSubH. mumkin ashuufak issaaʿa talaata.
kaamil	Tayyib. in sha'allaah. 'alfi shukr.

2 zeenab asked people in a hotel which languages they spoke. First, two girls ...

zeenab	inti bititkallimi lughaat 'eeh, min faDlik?
Girl	ana batkallim ʕárabi w ingiliizi shuwaỳya.
Girl	ana batkallim ʕárabi, batkallim ingiliizi shuwayya, mish kitiir.
zeenab	bititkallimi faransaawi?
Girl	la'.
zeenab	bititkallimi almaani?
Girl	la'.
zeenab	ʕárabi bass?
Girl	ʕárabi w ingiliizi shuwayya.

... then a man

zeenab	inta bititkallim lughaat 'eeh?
Man	ana batkallim ʕárabi w ingiliizi.
zeenab	bititkallim ingiliizi kwayyis walla nuSS nuSS walla shuwayya?
Man	shuwayya shuwayya!

3 Being introduced to someone at a party.

kaamil	misaa' ilkheer.
Hostess	misaa' innuur ... ahlan wa sahlan ... itfaDDalu ... sharraftuuna.
kaamil	shukran.
Hostess	ya duktuur saami, a'addimlak ilmuhandis kaamil Hasan, zimiili f ishshirka.
Dr saami	ahlan wa sahlan ... furSa saʕiida. itsharrafna.

4 Being offered a drink.

Hostess	tishrabu 'eeh ya gamaaʕa? fiih kull*i* Haaga.
leela	ashrab ʕaSiir lamuun min faDlik.
Hostess	w inta ya kaamil?
kaamil	ashrab biira min faDlik.

5 Are you happy in Cairo?

Host	inta mabSuuT fi maSr?
kaamil	'aywa, mabSuuT 'awi, innaas luTaaf giddan.
Host	w inti ya madaam?
leela	mabSuuTa 'awi, ilHamdu lillaah. bass ilgaww Harr shuwayya, mish kida?

6 Telling someone your plans.

kaamil	ʕandi maʕaad maʕa maHmuud makkaawi bukra. tiʕrafu?
Host	'aywa, raagil laTiif giddan. ilmaʕaad issaaʕa kam?
kaamil	issaaʕa khamsa w nuSS.
Host	inta w huwwa bass?
kaamil	la', ana w issayyid aHmad khaalid. raagil 'aʕmaal kuweeti.

7 Dinner is served!

Hostess	ʕaSiir taani, ya madaam?
leela	la', shukran, kifaaya kida.
Hostess	haniyyan ... il'akl gaahiz, ya gamaaʕa! itfaDDalu.

8 Asking someone to ring you.

kaamil	min faDlak, ya duktuur, kallimni yoom ilkhamiis iSSubH. nimrit tilifooni f ilbeet khamsa sabʕa talaata waaHid Sifr itneen. wi tilifoon ilmaktab, arbaʕa sitta tamanya khamsa waaHid waaHid.
Dr saami	Tayyib, in sha'allaah.

9 And farewells.

kaamil	Hafla mumtaaza, ya madaam. tislam ideeki. tiSbaHu ʕala kheer.
Hostess	tiSbaHu ʕala kheer.

Dr saami	ع andi sayyaara. mumkin awaSSalku?
kaamil	la', shukran. ilhutiil 'urayyib min hina.
Hostess	maعa ssalaama! maعa 'alf*i* salaama!

Vocabulary

mawguud *in, present*
sayyid *Mr*
maعaad *appointment*
'alf *a thousand*
bititkallim(i) *you speak*
batkallim *I speak*
عárabi *Arabic*
ingiliizi *English*
faransaawi *French*
almaani *German*
nuSS nuSS *so so*
zimiil (*pl* zamaayil) *colleague*
shirka (*pl* sharikaat) *company*
ya gamaaعa! *everybody*
kull*i* Haaga *everything*
mabSuuT *pleased, happy*
naas *people*
laTiif (*pl* luTaaf) *pleasant, kind*
giddan *very*
gaww *weather*
Harr *hot*
maعa *with*
aعraf *I know*
raagil (*pl* riggaala) *man*
raagil 'aعmaal *businessman*
kuweeti *Kuwaiti*
taani *another*
kifaaya *enough*
kida *like that, so*
haniyyan *with enjoyment*
gaahiz *ready*
'akl *food*
ilkhamiis *Thursday*
nimrit tilifoon *telephone number*
beet (*pl* buyuut) *house, home*
f ilbeet *at home*
Sifr *zero*
maktab *office*
Hafla *party, reception*
mumtaaz *lovely, splendid*
tislam ideeki *bless your hands*
sayyaara (*pl* sayyaraat) *car*
awaSSal *I give a lift*

Explanations

- To make an appointment with ...:
  mumkin aعmil maعaad maعa ...?
  to which you add the time, day, etc.

- To ask 'Do you know him?': **tiعrafu?**
  and 'Do you know her?': **tiعrafha?**

- **b**- or **bi**- is used before verbs if the action is ongoing or habitual
ana batkallim ƹárabi
bashrab biira I drink (*or* am drinking) beer

- **a'addim** means 'I introduce'.
With -**lak** *(m)* or -**lik** *(f)*, it means 'I introduce to you ...'
a'addimlak kaamil Hasan let me introduce kaamil Hasan to you *(talking to a man)*

- The imperative of **akallim** (I talk to) is **kallim. -ni** (me) can be added to it:
kallimni talk to me/call me

- More plurals

Adjectives, like nouns, have plural forms, but they are only used when referring to human beings.
luTaaf is the plural of **laTiif** (nice):
innaas luTaaf the people are nice

NB Plural nouns *not* referring to human beings take the *feminine singular* adjective:
issandwitshaat kwayyisa the sandwiches are nice
shikaat siyaHiyya travellers cheques

- **itfaDDalu** is the plural form of **itfaDDal** or **itfaDDali;** you might hear it when somebody is inviting everyone to come and eat.

- **tiSbaHu ƹala kheer** (good night) is the plural of **tiSbaH(i) ƹala kheer.**

- The commonest way of referring to a man politely is to use **issayyid** (Mr) followed by both his first and second names: **issayyid John Bates.** The equivalent term for a woman is **madaam,** and for a girl, **'anisa.**

idduktuur and **idduktuura** (Dr) are used before someone's first or second name.

il'ustaaz and **il'ustaaza** (*lit* Professor) are often used as a polite title for anyone with literary or academic qualifications.

Other job titles like **ilmuhandis** (engineer) are also used to introduce someone.

When addressing people, any of the following might be appropriate.

ya | **duktuur(a)**
| **'ustaaz(a)**
| **sayyid kamaal**
| **madaam**

Worth knowing

Social visits in Arab countries can involve a wealth of polite exchanges of welcome and appreciation, some of which have cropped up in previous chapters.

If you are invited home, you might well hear **sharraftuuna** (*lit* you have honoured us), which can be said at the beginning or the end of a visit.

When being introduced, a common expression is **furSa saɛiida** (pleased to meet you, *lit* a happy occasion), and also **itsharraft** (I am honoured) and **itsharrafna** (we are honoured).

In business dealings, a common way of wishing someone 'good luck' is **b ittawfiiq** (*lit* with success), not forgetting the usual **in sha'allaah.**

To thank someone and say you've had enough, say: **shukran, kifaaya kida.** The reply will often be: **haniyyan** (glad you enjoyed it, *lit* with enjoyment), which is used after either food or drink.

To compliment the hostess on her hospitality:
tislam iddeeki (*lit* bless your hands)

As you leave someone's home, you will often hear **nawwartu beetna** (you have brought light to our house) and **maʕa 'alfi salaama** (with a thousand goodbyes).

Additional vocabulary

miraati *my wife*
miraatak *your wife*
goozi *my husband*
goozik *your husband*
walad (*pl* 'awlaad) *son, child*
SaaHib (*pl* 'aSHaab) *friend (m)*
SaHba *friend* (f)

Exercises

1 You're making a phone call. Ask if the following people are in:

a the director
b Dr White
c Mr kamaal gindi
d Mrs zeenab

2 Which of the following expressions would you use A as a host or hostess, B as a guest?

a sharraftuuna A or B?
b tislam 'ideeki A or B?
c 'alf*i* shukr A or B?
d maʕa 'alfi salaama A or B?
e nawwartu beetna A or B?

3 Read the following dialogue aloud twice then answer the questions that follow.

Hostess misaa' ilkheer ya duktuur ashraf. ahlan wa sahlan. nawwart*i* beetna.
Guest ahlan biiki. izzayyik?
Hostess kwayyisa, ilHamdu lillaah ... itfaDDal ... tishrab 'eeh?

Guest	mayya maƐdaniyya bass, min faDlik.
Hostess	itfaDDal. tiƐraf issaayyid kh̲aalid gamaal, raagil 'aƐmaal min bag̲hdaad?
Guest	furSa saƐiida. its̲harraft.

a What time of day is it?
b Who has just arrived?
c What does he have to drink?
d Who is he introduced to?
e Where does the latter come from, and what's his job?

4 Ask a business acquaintance if you can see him ...:

a tomorrow
b tomorrow afternoon
c at half past four
d on Monday
e on Thursday morning
f the day after tomorrow
g in the hotel
h at home

Abu Simbel

Can you 'GET BY'?

When you have finished the course, try your hand at this test. There is a possible maximum score of 65 points. Check your answers on p80. You might like to keep a record of your score, try the test again after a few days and see if you have improved.

First contacts

1 Say 'good evening'.
2 Reply to SabaaH ilkheer.
3 Reply to ahlan wa sahlan.
4 Ask a woman how she is.
5 Ask a man when you'll see him.
6 Ask a woman where she's from.
7 Say you're from England.
8 Say you're not from here.
9 Say you're a student (female).
10 Say thank you very much.
11 Say goodnight (to a couple).

Eating and drinking

Ask for the following:
12 two coffees and a tea
13 the menu, please (to the waiter)
14 three orange juices
15 one chicken and two grilled fish
16 a cheese sandwich
17 a vegetable soup
18 the bill, please (to a waitress)

Now ask:
19 what sandwiches there are.
20 what juices he's got.
21 if there's any wine here.
22 where the restaurant is.
23 what time breakfast is.

Shopping

Ask the price of:

24 that galabiyya ...

25 ... and that red one

26 the large bag

27 a kilo of potatoes

28 four stamps for England

Say:

29 That bag is very expensive.

30 Can I see a bigger size?

31 I want to buy a film for this camera.

32 Have you got a map of Cairo? (to a man)

33 Impossible. That's very expensive (referring to a souvenir camel).

Out and about

Ask for:

34 A ticket to Aswan ...

35 ... second class ...

36 ... return.

Say:

37 I want to go to the pyramids (you're a man).

38 I want to go the day after tomorrow (you're a woman).

39 Is the museum near here?

40 Where's the nearest telephone?

41 Is there a plane in the afternoon?

42 Can I take a taxi?

43 Straight on here and second street on the left.

44 Is this the train for Port Said?

In a hotel

45 Ask the receptionist if he has a room with bath.

46 Say you haven't got a reservation.

47 Ask if you can make a phone call from here.

48 Say you want to change some sterling.

49 Say 'room number 213'.

50 Ask where the lavatory is.
51 Say you have travellers cheques.
52 Say the phone isn't working.
53 Say 'that's for you' (when tipping a man).

Social encounters

Ask:
54 What would you like to drink? (to a man)
55 Do you speak English? (to a woman)
56 Do you know Dr saami? (to a man)
57 Are you happy in London? (to a woman)
58 Another juice?

Say:
59 I have an appointment with Mr Hasan ...
60 ... at half past three.
61 Cairo is very big, isn't it?
62 What languages do you speak? (to a woman)
63 You speak a little Arabic ...
64 ... and French so so.

65 Finally, wish someone success.

Reference section

Language notes

- Nouns and adjectives

  il- is prefixed to definite nouns and adjectives:

'akl kwayyis	nice food
il'akl ilkwayyis	the nice food

- A final **-a** indicates the feminine:

mudarris laTiif	a nice teacher *(m)*
mudarrisa laTiifa	a nice teacher *(f)*

- Demonstratives (this/that/these/those)

  da *(m)*, **di** *(f)* and **dool** *(pl)* are added to definite nouns:

il'akl da	this/that food
ilmudiira di	this/that manageress
innaas dool	these/those people

  da, di and **dool** can be used by themselves when referring to masculine, feminine or plural nouns:

da kwayyis	that *(m)* is fine
di kibiira	that *(f)* one is big
dool min landan	those are from London

- Plurals

  -aat is often added to the singular:

  dolaar - **dolaraat** **sandwitsh** - **sandwitshaat**

  More usually the word changes internally, following one of half a dozen different 'patterns'. You just have to learn which plural pattern each noun takes.

  The commonest patterns:

kart	kuruut	'irsh	'uruush
shanTa	shunaT	furSa	furaS

maktab	makaatib	tazkara	tazaakir
maTᶜam	maTaa9im	sigaara	sagaayir
isbuuᶜ	asabiiᶜ	miftaaH	mafatiiH
SaaHib	'aSHaab	Sanf	'aSnaaf
walad	'awlaad	nooᶜ	'anwaaᶜ

After a plural noun a *feminine singular* adjective is usually used:

sandwitshaat kibiira big sandwiches

but the plural form of the adjective is used if the noun refers to human beings:

naas luTaaf nice people

This is a common pattern for plural adjectives:

Sughayyar Sughaar

- The dual

Instead of using the number 'two', the noun takes the 'dual' ending -**een:**

yoom day **yomeen** two days

In feminine nouns the -**a** ending changes to -**teen:**

Haaga thing **Hagteen** two things

When ordering food or drink, the singular noun is used with all numbers:

itneen biira two beers
arbaᶜa shaay four teas

- Comparatives and superlatives

The same basic pattern is used to make both the comparative (eg bigger) and superlative (eg biggest)

kibiir big **'akbar** bigger, biggest
rikhiiS cheap **'arkhaS** cheaper, cheapest

When it means 'bigger', 'cheaper' etc, it *follows* the noun:

Haaga 'arkhaS something cheaper

and it comes *before* the noun when it means 'biggest', 'cheapest', etc:

'arkhaS Haaga the cheapest thing

- Pronouns

As the subject of a sentence they take the following forms:

ana	I	**iHna**	we
inta	you *(m)*	**intu**	you *(pl)*
inti	you *(f)*		
huwwa	he	**humma**	they
hiyya	she		

Following a noun or preposition they take the forms:

-**i**	beet**i**	my home
-**ak**	beet**ak**	your *(m)* home
-**ik**	beet**ik**	your *(f)* home
-**u**	beet**u**	his home
-**ha**	beet**ha**	her home
-**na**	beet**na**	our home
-**ku**	beet**ku**	your *(pl)* home
-**hum**	beet**hum**	their home

After a preposition:
'uddaam**i** in front of me
ع**andu** *lit* with him, *ie* he has

After verbs, almost the same forms are used; only the 'me' form is different:
kallim speak to kallim**ni** speak to me

- A regular verb in the present tense:

ashrab	I drink	**nishrab**	we drink
tishrab	you *(m)* drink	**tishrabu**	you*(pl)* drink
tishrabi	you *(f)* drink		
yishrab	he drinks	**yishrabu**	they drink
tishrab	she drinks		

ie various prefixes and suffixes are added to the base **-shrab-**.
These forms can follow **mumkin** (can), **laazim** (must) and ع**aawiz** or ع**awza** (want):

mumkin ashrab?	can I drink?
laazim tishrab	you *(m)* must drink
ع**aawiz yishrab**	he wants to drink

- **bi**- precedes the verb if the action is habitual or ongoing:
  hiyya bitishrab mayya she (usually) drinks (*or* is now drinking) water
  bititkallim ingiliizi? do you speak English?

- Imperatives
  The initial **t**- of the second person is lost:
  ishrab! drink! *(m)*
  ishrabi! drink! *(f)*
  ishrabu! drink! *(pl)*

  For verbs like **ashuuf** (see) and **aruuH** (go), where the base begins with a single consonant, the initial -**i** is lost as well:
  shuuf! look! *(m)*
  shuufi! look! *(f)*
  shuufu! look! *(pl)*

- Negatives
  In 'verbless' sentences like
  ana min landan I (am) from London
  huwwa laTiif he (is) kind, pleasant
  mish is inserted:
  ana mish min landan
  huwwa mish laTiif etc

  With verbs, **ma**- and -**sh** are placed before and after the verb:
  mayishuufsh he doesn't see
  The same is true for **fiih** and **ɛand**-:
  mafiish 'akl there is no food
  maɛandiish sayyaara I don't have a car
  maɛandaksh sandwitshaat? don't you have sandwiches?

- Days of the week
  yoom litneen Monday
  yoom ittalaat Tuesday

yoom larbaع Wednesday
yoom ilkhamiis Thursday
yoom ilgumعa Friday
yoom issabt Saturday
yoom ilHadd Sunday
yoom (day) can be omitted.

- Months of the year

yanaayir	January	**yulyu**	July
fibraayir	February	**aghusTus**	August
maaris	March	**sibtimbir**	September
abriil	April	**uktuubar**	October
mayyu	May	**nuvimbir**	November
yunyu	June	**disimbir**	December

- The seasons

irrabiiع	the spring	**iSSeef**	the summer
ilkhariif	the autumn	**ishshita**	the winter

- Numbers

0	**Sifr**	14	**arbaعtaashar**
1	**waaHid**	15	**khamastaashar**
2	**itneen**	16	**sittaashar**
3	**talaata**	17	**sabعataashar**
4	**arbaعa**	18	**tamantaashar**
5	**khamsa**	19	**tisaعtaashar**
6	**sitta**	20	**عishriin**
7	**sabعa**	30	**talatiin**
8	**tamanya**	40	**arbiعiin**
9	**tisعa**	50	**khamsiin**
10	**عashara**	60	**sittiin**
11	**Hidaashar**	70	**sabعiin**
12	**itnaashar**	80	**tamaniin**
13	**talattaashar**	90	**tisعiin**

Any number over 10 is followed by a *singular* noun:
Hidaashar yoom 11 days
talatiin Taalib 30 students
To make numbers like twenty-five, fifty-three,

say 'five and twenty', 'three and fifty':

25 **khamsa w ع ishriin**

53 **talaata w khamsiin**

100	**miyya**	1000	**'alf**
200	**miteen**	2000	**'alfeen**
300	**tultumiyya**	3000	**talat alaaf**
400	**rubعumiyya**	4000	**arbaعt alaaf**
500	**khumsumiyya**	5000	**khamast alaaf**
600	**suttumiyya**	6000	**sitt alaaf**
700	**subعumiyya**	7000	**sabaعt alaaf**
800	**tumnumiyya**	8000	**tamant alaaf**
900	**tusعumiyya**	9000	**tisaعt alaaf**

When 100 - 900 are followed by a noun, -**miyya** becomes -**miit**:

£400	**rubعumiit gineeh**
300,000	**tultumiit 'alf**
400,000	**rubعumiit 'alf**

Key to exercises

Chapter 1

1 **a** ana min ingiltira.
b ismi John.

2 **a** ana min maSr. (*or* ana min ilqaahira).
b ismi Taari'.

3 **a** afternoon or evening.
b morning
c any time of day

4 **a** misaa' innuur.
b SabaaH innuur.
c ahlan biik(i).

5 **a** ahlan wa sahlan. ismak 'eeh?
b inta mineen?

6 **a** ahlan wa sahlan. ismik 'eeh?
b inti mineen?

7 **a** SabaaH ilkheer ya mu'nis.
b (inta) izzayyak?
c ashuufak imta?
d in sha'allaah.

Chapter 2

1 **a** عaSiir burTu'aan min faDlak.
b itneen biira min faDlak.
c sandwitsh min faDlak.
d 'ahwa maZbuuT min faDlak.
e shurbit khuDaar min faDlak.
f ilHisaab min faDlak.

2 min faDlak would become min faDlik.

3 **a** fiih 'ahwa?
b fiih عaSiir manga?
c fiih shurbit baSal?
d fiih ruzz?
e fiih sandwitshaat?

4 **a** عandak 'ahwa?
b عandak عaSiir manga?
c عandak shurbit baSal?
d عandak ruzz?
e عandak sandwitshaat?

5 **a** عandak sandwitshaat gibna?
b fiih nibiit hina?
c عandak mayya maعdaniyya?
d ilHisaab min faDlak.
e shukran.

Chapter 3

1 **a** a big bag
b the big bag
c the bag is big
d this bag is big

2 **a** عandak kuruut buSTaal min faDlak?
b عandak Tawaabiع min faDlak?
c عandak film mulawwan min faDlak?
d عandak shanTa kibiira min faDlak?
e عandak gallabiyya Hamra?

3 **a** mumkin ashuuf gallabiyya?
b mumkin ashuuf ilkamera di?
c mumkin ashuuf ma'aas 'akbar?
d mumkin ashuuf Sanf 'arkhaS?

4 **a** bi kam kiilu ilburTu'aan?
b bi kam nuSS kiilu illamuun?
c bi kam itneen kiilu ilmooz?
d bi kam nuSS kiilu issukkar?

5 **a** di ghalya 'awi
b da ghaali 'awi
c da ghaali 'awi
d di ghalya 'awi

6 **a** fiih shanTa 'akbar?
b fiih fustaan 'aSghar?
c fiih kamera 'arkhaS?
d fiih Sanf 'aHsan?

Chapter 4

1 **a** fiih Hammaam?
b fiih dushsh?
c fiih tilifoon?
d fiih mayya sukhna?

2 **a** ilHammaam ع aTlaan.
b iddushsh ع aTlaan.
c ittilifoon ع aTlaan.
d mafiish mayya sukhna.

3 **a** mumkin adfa ع ilHisaab?
b mumkin a ع mil tilifoon?
c mumkin aghayyar dolaraat?

4 SabaaH innuur.
fiih 'ooDa faDya?
bi siriir waaHid.
lelteen.
bi kam il'ooDa?

Chapter 5

1 ع aawiz ... (*or* ع awza ...)
a aakhud taksi.
b aruuH ilharam.
c aruuH il'utiil.
d aruuH ilmatHaf.
e tazkara li 'aSwaan.

2 laazim ...
a taakhud taksi.
b tishuuf ilharam.
c tidfa ع ilHisaab.
d tiruuH il'agzakhaana.

3 laazim
a takhdi taksi
b tishuufi ilharam.
c tidfa ع i ilHisaab.
d tiruuHi il'agzakhaana

4 **a** (imshi) ع ala Tool.
b (imshi) ع ala shshimaal.
c (taakhuud) 'awwil shaari ع ع ala lyimiin.

5 (ana) ʕaawiz aruuH 'aSwaan.
dáraga 'uula.
raayiH gayy.
itfaDDal.

6 **a** 5.30 **b** 2.15 **c** 10.20 **d** 2.55 **e** 12.45

Chapter 6

1
a ilmudiir mawguud?
b idduktuur White mawguud?
c issayyid kamaal gindi mawguud?
d madaam zeenab mawguuda?

2 **a** A **b** B **c** B **d** A or B **e** A

3
a afternoon or evening
b Dr ashraf
c mineral water
d Mr khaalid gamaal
e He's a businessman from Baghdad.

4 mumkin ashuufak ...
a bukra?
b bukra baʕd iDDuhr?
c issaaʕa arbaʕa w nuSS?
d (yoom) litneen?
e (yoom) ilkhamiis iSSubH?
f baʕd bukra?
g f il'utiil?
h f ilbeet?

Answers to 'Can you get by?'

1 misaa' ilkheer.
2 SabaaH innuur.
3 ahlan biik (to a man); ahlan biiki (to a woman)
4 izzayyik?
5 ashuufak imta?
6 inti mineen?
7 ana min ingiltira.
8 ana mish min hina.
9 ana Taaliba.
10 'alf shukr.
11 tiSbaHu ɛala kheer.
12 itneen 'ahwa w waaHid shaay.
13 ilminyu, min faDlak.
14 talaata ɛaSiir burTu'aan.
15 waaHid firaakh w itneen samak mashwi.
16 (waaHid) sandwitsh gibna.
17 (waaHid) shurbit khuDaar.
18 ilHisaab, min faDlik.
19 fiih sandwitshaat 'eeh?
20 ɛandak ɛaSiir 'eeh?
21 fiih nibiit hina?
22 ilmaTɛam feen?
23 ilfiTaar issaaɛa kam?
24 bi kam ilgallabiyya di ...?
25 ... w ilHamra di?
26 bi kam ishshanTa ilkibiira?
27 bi kam kiilu ilbaTaaTis?
28 bi kam arbaɛ Tawaabiɛ l ingiltira?
29 ishshanTa di ghalya 'awi.
30 mumkin ashuuf ma'aas 'akbar?
31 ɛaawiz (*or* ɛawza) film l ilkámera di?
32 ɛandak khariiTa l ilqaahira?
33 mish mumkin. da ghaali 'awi.
34 tazkara li 'aSwaan
35 ...dáraga tanya
36 ...raayiH gayy.
37 ɛaawiz aruuH ilharam.
38 ɛawza aruuH baɛd bukra.
39 ilmatHaf 'urayyib min hina?
40 feen 'a'rab tilifoon?
41 fiih Tayyaara iDDuhr?
42 mumkin aakhud taksi?
43 ɛala Tool hina wi taani shaariɛ ɛala shshimaal.
44 da 'aTr buur saɛiid?
45 ɛandak 'ooDa bi Hammaam?
46 maɛandiish Hagz.
47 mumkin aɛmil tilifoon min hina?

48 ana ɛaawiz (*or* ɛawza) aghayyar istirliini.
49 'ooDa nimra miteen wi talataashar.
50 ittwalett feen?
51 ɛandi shikaat siyaHiyya.
52 ittilifoon ɛaTlaan (*or* mish shaghghaal).
53 da ɛalashaanak.
54 tishrab 'eeh?
55 (inti) bititkallimi ingiliizi?
56 (inta) tiɛraf idduktuur saami?
57 (inti) mabSuuTa fi landan?
58 ɛaSiir taani?
59 ɛandi maɛaad maɛa issayyid Hasan …
60 … issaaɛa talaata w nuSS.
61 ilqaahira kibiira 'awi, mish kida? (*or* maSr kibiira, mish kida?)
62 (inti) bititkallimi lughaat 'eeh?
63 (ana) batkallim ɛárabi shuwayya …
64 … wi faransaawi nuSS nuSS.
65 b ittawfiiq, in sha'allaah.

Word list

The following is a list of the words appearing in the conversations in the six chapters.
The alphabetical order used is:
' a b d D e f g gh h H i k kh l m n o q r s S sh t T u v w y z Z ع

In addition, related forms are shown thus wherever they seem valuable:

plurals Suura (*pl* Suwar)
masculines Hamra (*m* 'aHmar)
feminines gaahiz (*f* gahza)

Verbs are given in the first person singular form, eg
ashtiri I buy
ashuuf I see
so if you are looking for the words tishrab or tiعraf, look under ashrab or aعraf. A fuller list of verb forms can be found on p73-74.

'

'a'rab *nearer, nearest*
'aasif (*f* 'asfa) *sorry*
'agzakhaana *chemist*
'ahwa *coffee*
'aHsan *better, best*
'akbar *bigger, biggest*
'akl *food*
'alf *a thousand*
'alf shukr *many thanks*
'alo *hallo* (on phone)
'arkhaS *cheaper; cheapest*
'asanSiir *lift*
'asfa *sorry* (f)
'aSwaan *Aswan*
'aTr *train*
'awi *very*
'awwil (*f* 'uula) *first*
'aywa *yes*
'eeh? *what?*
'irsh (*pl* 'uruush) *piastre*
'izaaza *bottle*
'ooDa (*pl* 'owaD) *room*
'uddaam *in front of*
'umaash *material*
'urayyib (min) *near (to)*
'uruush *piastres*
'utiil *hotel*
'uula *first* (f)

a

a'addimlak ... *let me introduce ... to you*
aakul *I eat*
aakhud *I take*
adfaع *I pay*
aghayyar *I change*
ahlan *hallo, nice to meet you*
ahlan biik(i) *reply to* ahlan or ahlan wa sahlan
ahlan wa sahlan *hallo, nice to meet you, welcome*
akallim *I speak (to)*
aktib *I write*
almaani *German*
amDi *I sign*
amshi *I go*
ana *I*
arbaعa *four*
arbiعiin *forty*

aruuH *I go (to)*
ashrab *I drink*
ashtiri *I buy*
ashuuf *I see*
atkallim *I speak*
awaSSal *I give a lift*
ayyi khidma *can I help you?; don't mention it*
aع mil tilifoon *I make a phone call*
aعraf *I know*

b
balad *town, country*
bank *bank*
banyu *bath*
babuur *passport*
bass *but; only*
baSal *onion*
batkallim *I speak*
baTaaTis *potatoes*
baعd *after*
baعd bukra *(the) day after tomorrow*
baعdeen *later, then*
baعd iDDuhr *afternoon*
beeD *eggs*
beet (*pl* buyuut) *house, home*
bi *with*
bi balaash *free, for nothing*
bi kam? *how much?*
bi kheer *fine, well*
bi kull suruur *with the greatest pleasure; certainly*
biira *beer*
bisilla *peas*
biعiid (min) *far (from)*
bukra *tomorrow*
burTu'aan *orange*
buur saعiid *Port Said*

d
da *this, that* (m)
dáraga *class*
di *this, that* (f)
di'ii'a *moment, minute*
dilwa'ti *now*
dolaar (*pl* dolaraat) *dollar*
door *floor*
duktuur (*f* -a) *doctor*
dushsh *shower*

D
Duhr *(after)noon*

f
faaDi (*f* faDya) *empty, free*
falaafil *chick peas or beans*
faransaawi *French*
farawla *strawberry*
feen? *where?*
fi *in, at*
fiih *there is/are*
film (*pl* 'aflaam) *film*
firaakh *chicken*
fiTaar *breakfast*
furSa saعiida *pleased to meet you*
fuul *cooked beans*

g
gaahiz (*f* gahza) *ready*
gallabiyya (*pl* -aat) *galabiyya*
gamaaعa *everyone*
gamal *camel*
gambari *prawns*
gawaafa *guava*
gaww *weather*
gibna *cheese*
giddan *very*
gineeh *pound*
grepfruut *grapefruit*

gh
ghaali (*f* ghalya) *expensive*

h
haniyyan *glad you enjoyed it*
haram *pyramids*
hina *here*
hinaak *there*
hiyya *she*
hutiil *hotel*
huwwa *he*

H
HaaDir *certainly, at once*
Haaga (*pl* Hagaat) *thing, something*

Haaga kamaan? (*or* Haaga tanya?) *anything else?*
Hafla (*pl* Hafalaat) *party, reception*
Hagz *reservation*
Hammaam *bathroom*
Hamra (*m* 'aHmar) *red*
Harr *hot*
Hilw *beautiful, fine, sweet*
Hisaab *bill*

i
iddiini *give me*
ilHamdu lillaah *fine (God be praised)*
ilkhamiis *Thursday*
ilkhartuum *Khartoum*
illa *less, without*
ilqaahira *Cairo*
ilʿafw *not at all; don't mention it*
imta? *when?*
ingiliizi *English*
ingiltira *England*
in sha'allaah *God willing; I hope so*
inta *you* (m)
inti *you* (f)
iskindriyya *Alexandria*
ism *name*
issaaʿa kam? *what time is it?; at what time?*
issudaan *Sudan*
issuʿudiyya *Saudi Arabia*
istirliini *sterling*
iSSumaal *Somalia*
itfaDDal(i) *here you are; help yourself*
itnaashar *twelve*
itneen *two*
izzayyak? *how are you* (to a man)
izzayyik? *how are you?* (to a woman)

k
kallimni *ring me*
kam? *how much?; how many?*
kamaan *also*
kámera *camera*
kart (*pl* kuruut) buSTaal *postcard*
kibiir *big*
kibda *liver*
kida *like that, so*
kifaaya *enough*
kitiir *a lot, much, many*
kufta *meat balls*
kull *each, every*
kuweeti *Kuwaiti*
kwayyis *fine, well*

kh
khamsa *five*
khan ilkhaliili *Khan El Khalili*
khariiTa *map*
khidma *service*
khuDaar *vegetables*

l
la' *no*
laazim *it is necessary, have to, must*
lamuun *lemon*
landan *London*
laTiif (*pl* luTaaf) *nice, pleasant*
leela (*pl* layaali) *night*
li *to, for*
litneen *Monday*
lugha (*pl* -aat) *language*

m
ma'aas *size*
mabSuuT *happy*
mafiish *there isn't/aren't*
maktab (*pl* makaatib) *office*
malyaan *full*
manga *mango*
maSr *Egypt, Cairo* (see p19)
mashwi *grilled*
matHaf *museum*
maTʿam (*pl* maTaaʿim) *restaurant*
mawguud *available, in*
mayya (maʿdaniyya) *(mineral) water*
maZbuuT *right; exact;*

medium sweet
maعa *with*
maعa ssalaama *goodbye*
maعaad *appointment*
maعandiish *I haven't*
midaan *square*
midaan ittaHriir *Liberation Square*
min *from*
mineen? *where from?*
min faDlak *please* (to a man)
min faDlik *please* (to a woman)
minyu *menu*
misaa' ilkheer *good afternoon/evening*
misaa' innuur *reply to* misaa' ilkheer
mish *not*
mish kida? *isn't it?; isn't that so?*
miteen *two hundred*
mitr *metre*
mudarris *(f* -a) *teacher*
mudiir (*f* -a) *manager, director*
muftaaH *key*
muhandis (*f* -a) *engineer*
mulawwan *coloured, in colour*
mumkin *it is possible*
mumtaaz *lovely, splendid*

n
naas *people*
nawwartu beetna *you have honoured us*
nibiit *wine*
nimra *number*
nimrit tilifoon *telephone number*
nuSS *half*
nuSS nuSS *so so*
nuuba *Nubia*

r
raagil (*pl* riggaala) *man*
raagil 'aعmaal *businessman*
raayiH *single*
raayiH gayy *return*
raSiif *platform*
rikhiiS *cheap*
rubع *quarter*
ruzz *rice*

s
sa'عa *cold*
saaعa *hour; time*
sabaanikh *spinach*
sabعa *seven*
sabعiin *seventy*
samak *fish*
sanduu' *box*
sandwitsh (*pl* -aat) *sandwich*
sayyaara (*pl* sayyaraat) *car*
sayyid *Mr*
siriir *bed*
sitta *six*
sittiin *sixty*
sukhna *hot*
suttumiyya *six hundred*

S
SabaaH ilkheer *good morning*
SabaaH innuur *reply to* SabaaH ilkheer
Sanf (*pl* 'aSnaaf) *kind, sort*
Sifr *zero*
SubH *morning*
Suura (*pl* Suwar) *picture*

sh
shaariع (*pl* shawaariع) *street*
shaay *tea*
shanTa (*pl* shunaT) *bag*
sharraftuuna *you have honoured us*
shiik (*pl* shikaat) siyaHiyya *travellers cheque*
shiisha *hubble bubble*
shimaal *left*
shirka (*pl* sharikaat) *company*
shukran *thank you*
shurba *soup*
shuwayya *a little, quite*

t
taani (*f* tanya) *second; other*
taksi (*pl* taksiyyaat) *taxi*
talaata *three*

talatiin *thirty*
taman *cost, price*
tamanya *eight*
tanya *second* (f)
tazkara (*pl* tazaakir) *ticket*
tiSbaH ع ala kheer *good night*
tilifoon *telephone*
tilivizyoon *television*
tilt *a third; twenty minutes*
tislam ideeki *thank you for your hospitality (lit bless your hands)*

T

Taabiع (*pl* Tawaabiع) *stamp*
Taalib (*f* -a) *student*
Tabعan *of course*
Tayyaara (*pl* Tayyaraat) *aeroplane*
Tayyib *OK, well now ...*
Taعmiyya *fried cakes of ground beans*

w

waaHid (*f* waHda) *one*
walla *or*
wi *and*

y

ya *form of address* (see p17)
y afandim *sir*
ya beeh *sir*
ya madaam *madam*
yimiin *right*
yoom (*pl* 'ayyaam) *day*

z

zimiil (*pl* zamaayil) *colleague*

ع

عaawiz (*or* عaayiz) *I/you/he want(s)*
عafwan *not at all; don't mention it*
عala *on*
عala Tool *straight on*
عalashaan *for*
عandi *I have*
عárabi *Arabic*
عaSiir *juice*
عaTlaan *not working*
عawza (*or* عayza) *I/you/she want(s)*
عishriin *twenty*

An introduction to Arabic writing

The purpose of this section is to help you recognise public signs, posters, notices and the like which you will see on visits to Arab countries.

Arabic is written from right to left, and its alphabet has 29 letters. Most of these letters are easy to pronounce for English speakers, as equivalent sounds exist in English (see Pronunciation guide, p8). The Arabic alphabet and the corresponding transliterations are as follows:

NB 'th' is pronounced as in 'thanks' and 'th' as in 'that'

kh	H	j or g	th	t	b	a	'glottal stop
خ	ح	ج	ث	ت	ب	أ	ء

D	S	sh	s	z	r	th	d
ض	ص	ش	س	ز	ر	ذ	د

k	q	f	gh	ع	Z	T
ك	ق	ف	غ	ع	ظ	ط

y	w	h	n	m	l
ي	و	هـ	ن	م	ل

These three letters are used as long vowels:
aa ا ii ي *or* يـ uu و

The glottal stop ء is usually 'carried' on top of one of the long vowel symbols; eg أ = 'a

NB The sound represented by ذ (as in 'that') has changed into 'd' or 'z' in spoken Egyptian Arabic, and the sound represented by ث (as in 'thanks') has changed into 't' or 's'.

There are vowel 'marks' which are not included in the 29 letters of the alphabet. They *can* be shown, written above or below the consonant (eg تَ = ta, تِ = ti, تُ = tu), but in writing and print the marks are nearly always omitted, (a bit like English shorthand) as those who know the language well can recognise the words without them.

If a consonant is doubled, a ّ appears above the letter: (eg حمّام = Hammaam, ستّة = sitta).

Unlike English, Arabic letters are 'joined up' into words not only in writing but in print as well. The 'joining' system, however, is subject to certain rules to avoid risk of confusion and also for aesthetic purposes (Arabs are very proud of the beauty of the Arabic script).

1 The following letters never join the letter following them.

ا أ د ذ ر ز و

2 The following letters 'shrink' when they are joined up, ie they become narrower.

ب ت ث ي ن ف ق

3 The following letters lose their tails or 'flourishes' when they join. The letters are still easily recognisable after their tails are cut.

ج ح خ س ش ص ض ع غ ل

4 The final letter in all words is written in full, that is to say, it retains its original shape as given in the alphabet list above.

5 The following table shows those letters that change depending on whether they come at the beginning, in the middle or at the end of a word.

End	Middle	Beginning
ـة ة ت	ـتـ	تـ
ع ـع	ـعـ	عـ
غ ـغ	ـغـ	غـ
ـك	ـكـ	كـ
ـه ه	ـهـ	هـ
ى ـي	ـيـ	يـ

NB ة is a feminine ending, so it is always a final letter. If joined to the previous letter, it is ـة . The final letter ى can stand for a final 'a'.

The following shows how separate letters join together to form words according to the above rules. We have used each letter in the three possible positions - beginning, middle and end. Translations are not given as the words are intended simply as examples of the appearance of the writing system. Remember, you are reading from right to left.

a	أ	أ ك ل أكل	س أ ل سأل	ب د أ بدأ
b	ب	ب يـ ت بيت	س ب ت سبت	ك ت ب كتب
t	ت	ت يـ ن تين	ك ت ب كتب	ب ن ت بنت
t	ة	ق ـهـ و ة قهوة	ـة	حفلة
th	ث	ث ل ج ثلج	ن ث ر نثر	ل ب ث لبث
j/g	ج	ج م ل جمل	س ج د سجد	ن ت ج نتج
H	ح	ح ر ب حرب	ب ح ر بحر	ل م ح لمح
<u>kh</u>	خ	خ ب ز خبز	د خ ل دخل	ص ر خ صرخ
d	د	د خ ل دخل	ب د ر بدر	ب ل د بلد
<u>th</u>	ذ	ذ هـ ب ذهب	ب ذ ر بذر	ل ذ يـ ذ لذيذ
r	ر	ر ج ل رجل	ب ر د برد	أ ج ر أجر

z	ز	ز ي ت زيت	ن ز ف نزف	ب ر ز برز
s	س	س ت ر ستر	م س ك مسك	ل م س لمس
sh	ش	ش ك ر شكر	ر ش د رشد	ق ر ش قرش
S	ص	ص ر ف صرف	م ص ر مصر	ح ر ص حرص
D	ض	ض ي ف ضيف	ن ض ر نضر	ع ر ض عرض
T	ط	ط ر ب طرب	ق ط ر قطر	ن ف ط نفط
Z	ظ	ظ ب ي ظبي	ن ظ ر نظر	و ع ظ وعظ
ع	ع	ع ل م علم	س ع د سعد	م ن ع ب ر ع منع برع
gh	غ	غ ر ب غرب	ب غ د ا د بغداد	ب ل غ ف ر غ بلغ فرغ
f	ف	ف ت ح فتح	ل ف ت لفت	أ ل ف ألف
q	ق	ق ل ب قلب	ن ق ل نقل	ح ل ق حلق

k	ك	ك ت ب	م ك ت ب	س م ك	
		كتب	مكتب	سمك	
l	ل	ل ب س	ب ل د	ح م ل	
		لبس	بلد	حمل	
m	م	م ل ك	س م ك	ق ل م	
		ملك	سمك	قلم	
n	ن	ن ش ر	ب ن ت	ل ب ن	
		نشر	بنت	لبن	
h	هـ	هـ ر م	س هـ ل	ر ف ه	ب ل د ه
		هرم	سهل	رفه	بلده
w	و	و ل د	ف و ل	ح ل و	
		ولد	فول	حلو	
y	ي	يـ ج د	ن يـ ل	ل ق ي	هـ د ى
		يجد	نيل	لقي	هدى

Here is a list of some of the words and phrases you will be most likely to see on signs and notices. They are given with (a) a 'spoken' form following the transliteration system explained on pp8-10 and (b) an English translation.

menu	ilminyu	المنيو
restaurant	maTعam	مطعم
hotel	hutiil	هوتيل
hotel	funduq	فندق
WC	doorit mayya	دورة مياه

gents	l irrigaal	للرجال
ladies	l issayyidaat	للسيّدات
danger	khaTar	خطر
exit	khuruug	خروج
no entry	mamnuuع iddukhuul	ممنوع الدخول
no smoking	mamnuuع ittadkhiin	ممنوع التدخين
no photographs	mamnuuع ittaSwiir	ممنوع التصوير
no parking	mamnuuع wuquuf issayyaraat	ممنوع وقوف السيّارات
bus stop	mawqaf il'utubiis	موقف الأوتوبيس
taxi rank	mawqaf ittaksi	موقف التاكسي
car park	mawqaf issayyaraat	موقف السيارات
post office	maktab ilbariid	مكتب البريد
information office	maktab ilistiعlamaat	مكتب الاستعلامات
information	ilistiعlamaat	الاستعلامات
tourist office	maktab issiyaaHa	مكتب السياحة
ticket window	shibbaak ittazaakir	شبّاك التذاكر
bank	maSraf	مصرف

bank	bank	بنك
bureau de change	maSraf taghyiir ilعumla	مصرف تغيير العملة
bureau de change	maktab Siraafa	مكتب صرافة
to the airport	ila lmaTaar	إلى المطار
to the station	ila lmaHaTTa	إلى المحطة
stop	qif	قف
customs	ilgamaarik	الجمارك
passports and visas	ilgawazaat w itta'shiiraat	الجوازات والتأشيرات
embassy	sifaara	سفارة
consulate	qunSuliyya	قنصليّة
museum	matHaf	متحف
exhibition	maعraD	معرض
company	shirka	شركة
telephone	ittilifoon	التيليفون
|telephone	ilhaatif	الهاتف]
telephones	tilifoonaat	تيليفونات
telegrams	tilighrafaat	تليغرافات
hospital	mustashfa	مستشفى
chemist's	'agzakhaana	أجزخانة
chemist's	Saydaliyya	صيدليّة
police station	qism ilbuliis	قسم البوليس

police station	markaz ishshurTa	] مركز الشرطة
cafe	maqha	مقهى

In much of the Arab world, the following figures are used:

٩	٨	٧	٦	٥	٤	٣	٢	١	٠
9	8	7	6	5	4	3	2	1	0

Compound numbers are written from left to right as in English.

٧٨٦٤٣١٥	ت ٣٥١٤٧٦	١٩٨٥
7 8 6 4 3 1 5	Tel: 3 5 1 4 7 6	1985

NB In north-west Africa, the original (Arabic!) numbers have been retained: 1, 2, 3 ...

NOTES

NOTES